Beginning C# 7 Hands-On – Advanced Language Features

Learn the advanced-level features of C# 7 using Visual Studio 2017

Tom Owsiak

BIRMINGHAM - MUMBAI

Beginning C# 7 Hands-On – Advanced Language Features

First published: October 2017

Production reference: 1271017

Published by Packt Publishing Ltd.
Livery Place
35 Livery Street
Birmingham
B3 2PB, UK.
ISBN 978-1-78829-426-3

www.packtpub.com

Credits

Author
Tom Owsiak

Copy Editor
Tom Jacob

Project Editor
Suzanne Coutinho

Proofreader
Safis Editing

Acquisition Editor
Dominic Shakeshaft

Indexer
Pratik Shirodkar

Content Development Editor
Gary Schwartz

Graphics
Kirk D'Penha

Technical Editor
Gaurav Gavas

Production Coordinator
Arvindkumar Gupta

About the Author

Tom Owsiak has eight years of experience as a teacher in Mathematics, Physics, Statistics, and Programming. He has worked for five years as a database programmer using various technologies such as .NET, Clipper, SQL, SQL Server, SAS, and Excel, and many related technologies.

Tom is the publisher of one of the most successful courses on Udemy, called *Learn C# With Visual Studio 2013*. Currently, Tom works as a Mathematics and Computer Science teacher at Mercy College in Dobbs Ferry, NY.

www.PacktPub.com

For support files and downloads related to your book, please visit www.PacktPub.com. Did you know that Packt offers eBook versions of every book published, with PDF and ePub files available? You can upgrade to the eBook version at www.PacktPub.com and as a print book customer, you are entitled to a discount on the eBook copy. Get in touch with us at service@packtpub.com for more details. At www.PacktPub.com, you can also read a collection of free technical articles, sign up for a range of free newsletters and receive exclusive discounts and offers on Packt books and eBooks.

https://www.packtpub.com

Get the most in-demand software skills with Mapt. Mapt gives you full access to all Packt books and video courses, as well as industry-leading tools to help you plan your personal development and advance your career.

Why subscribe?

- Fully searchable across every book published by Packt
- Copy and paste, print, and bookmark content
- On demand and accessible via a web browser

Customer Feedback

Thanks for purchasing this Packt book. At Packt, quality is at the heart of our editorial process. To help us improve, please leave us an honest review on this book's Amazon page at `https://www.amazon.com/dp/1788294262`.

If you'd like to join our team of regular reviewers, you can email us at `customerreviews@packtpub.com`. We award our regular reviewers with free eBooks and videos in exchange for their valuable feedback. Help us be relentless in improving our products!

Table of Contents

Preface

Beginning C# 7 Hands-On – Advanced Language Features assumes that you've mastered the basic elements of the C# language and that you're now ready to learn the more advanced C# language and syntax, line by line, in a working Visual Studio environment. You'll learn how to code advanced C# language topics including generics, lambda expressions, and anonymous methods. You'll learn to use query syntax to construct queries and deploy queries that perform aggregation functions. You'll work with C# 7 and SQL Server 2017 to perform complex joins and stored procedures. Explore advanced file access methods, and see how to serialize and deserialize objects—all by writing working lines of code that you can run within Visual Studio. You'll also take a look at C# through web programming with web forms. By the time you've finished this book, you'll know all the critical advanced elements of the C# language and how to program everything from C# generics to XML, LINQ, and your first full MVC web applications. These are the advanced building blocks that you can then combine to exploit the full power of the C# programming language, line by line. This book is designed for beginner C# developers who have mastered the basics now, and for anyone who needs a fast reference to using advanced C# language features in practical coding examples.

What you need for this book

Visual Studio 2017, which will install and run on Windows 7 or above, and 2 GB or 4 GB of RAM is recommended. A minimum 20-50 GB of hard disk space is essential for typical installations.

Who this book is for

This book will appeal to anyone who is interested in learning how to program in C#. Previous programming experience will help you get through the initial sections with ease, although it's not mandatory to possess any experience at all.

Conventions

In this book, you will find a number of text styles that distinguish between different kinds of information. Here are some examples of these styles and an explanation of their meaning. Code words in text, database table names, folder names, filenames, file extensions, path names, dummy URLs, user input, and Twitter handles are shown as follows: "Specifically, `Default.aspx` is a file that contains the markup of the elements on the web page."

A block of code is set as follows:

```
<asp:DropDownList ID="DropDownList1" runat="server" AutoPostBack="True">
    <asp:ListItem>Monday</asp:ListItem>
    <asp:ListItem>Tuesday</asp:ListItem>
    <asp:ListItem>Wednesday</asp:ListItem>
</asp:DropDownList>
```

When we wish to draw your attention to a particular part of a code block, the relevant lines or items are set in bold:

```
<asp:DropDownList ID="DropDownList1" runat="server" AutoPostBack="True">
    <asp:ListItem>Monday</asp:ListItem>
    <asp:ListItem>Tuesday</asp:ListItem>
    <asp:ListItem>Wednesday</asp:ListItem>
</asp:DropDownList>
```

New terms and **important words** are shown in bold. Words that you see on the screen, for example, in menus or dialog boxes, appear in the text like this: "If you wish, click on **Browse** and save the file to a location you choose and click on **OK**."

Warnings or important notes appear like this.

Tips and tricks appear like this.

Reader feedback

Feedback from our readers is always welcome. Let us know what you think about this book—what you liked or disliked. Reader feedback is important for us as it helps us develop titles that you will really get the most out of. To send us general feedback, simply email feedback@packtpub.com, and mention the book's title in the subject of your message. If there is a topic that you have expertise in and you are interested in either writing or contributing to a book, see our author guide at www.packtpub.com/authors.

Customer support

Now that you are the proud owner of a Packt book, we have a number of things to help you to get the most from your purchase.

Downloading the example code

You can download the example code files for this book from your account at http://www.packtpub.com. If you purchased this book elsewhere, you can visit http://www.packtpub.com/support and register to have the files emailed directly to you. You can download the code files by following these steps:

1. Log in or register to our website using your email address and password.
2. Hover the mouse pointer on the **SUPPORT** tab at the top.
3. Click on **Code Downloads & Errata**.
4. Enter the name of the book in the **Search** box.
5. Select the book for which you're looking to download the code files.
6. Choose from the drop-down menu where you purchased this book from.
7. Click on **Code Download**.

Once the file is downloaded, please make sure that you unzip or extract the folder using the latest version of:

- WinRAR / 7-Zip for Windows
- Zipeg / iZip / UnRarX for Mac
- 7-Zip / PeaZip for Linux

The code bundle for the book is also hosted on GitHub at `https://github.com/PacktPublishing/Beginning-CSharp-7-Hands-On-Advanced-Language-Features`. We also have other code bundles from our rich catalog of books and videos available at `https://github.com/PacktPublishing/`. Check them out!

Downloading the color images of this book

We also provide you with a PDF file that has color images of the screenshots/diagrams used in this book. The color images will help you better understand the changes in the output. You can download this file from `https://www.packtpub.com/sites/default/files/downloads/BeginningCSharp7HandsOnAdvancedLanguageFeatures_ColorImages.pdf`.

Errata

Although we have taken every care to ensure the accuracy of our content, mistakes do happen. If you find a mistake in one of our books—maybe a mistake in the text or the code—we would be grateful if you could report this to us. By doing so, you can save other readers from frustration and help us improve subsequent versions of this book. If you find any errata, please report them by visiting `http://www.packtpub.com/submit-errata`, selecting your book, clicking on the **Errata Submission Form** link, and entering the details of your errata. Once your errata are verified, your submission will be accepted and the errata will be uploaded to our website or added to any list of existing errata under the Errata section of that title. To view the previously submitted errata, go to `https://www.packtpub.com/books/content/support` and enter the name of the book in the search field. The required information will appear under the **Errata** section.

Piracy

Piracy of copyrighted material on the internet is an ongoing problem across all media. At Packt, we take the protection of our copyright and licenses very seriously. If you come across any illegal copies of our works in any form on the internet, please provide us with the location address or website name immediately so that we can pursue a remedy. Please contact us at `copyright@packtpub.com` with a link to the suspected pirated material. We appreciate your help in protecting our authors and our ability to bring you valuable content.

Questions

If you have a problem with any aspect of this book, you can contact us at
`questions@packtpub.com`, and we will do our best to address the problem.

1
Creating a Simple Generics Class

In this chapter, you will look at the basics of making a simple generic class so that one class can operate on many different data types. A great benefit of generics is flexibility.

Creating a generics class

Bring up a project, and go to **Solution Explorer**; right-click, select **Add**, and click on **Class**. Name the class GenericsClass; a simple generics class. Then, click on **OK**. When the Visual Studio message comes up, click on **Yes**.

For our purposes, you don't need any of the using System lines at the top, nor any of the comments underneath, so delete them. Your initial screen should look like *Figure 1.1.1*:

```
1 public class GenericsClass
2 {
3     public GenericsClass()
4     {
5
6     }
7 }
```

Figure 1.1.1: The initial GenericsClass.cs screen

Working with different data types

Now, let's put a `<T>` symbol after where it says `public class GenericsClass`, as follows:

```
public class GenericsClass<T>
```

This means that this single class can work equally well with several different data types. Next, enter the following beneath the open curly brace under the preceding line:

```
private T[] vals;
```

Enter the following comment directly above this line:

```
//generic array instance variable
```

In other words, this will operate equally well on doubles, decimals, integers, and so on.

Making parameters that are generic

Now, in the following line, enter the following:

```
public GenericsClass(T[] input)
```

As you can see, you can also make parameters that are generic like this one. This is a parameter, `input` is the name of it, and the type is `T`. So, it's a generic array.

Next, enter the following between a set of curly braces beneath the preceding line:

```
vals = input;
```

Displaying the values

Of course, you should be able to display these values. so, enter the following line beneath the closed curly brace under the `vals = input;` line:

```
public string DisplayValues()
```

To display these values, you'll enter the following between a set of curly braces beneath the preceding line.

First, put in a string, as follows:

```
string str = null;
```

Next, declare the string and initialize the value to null.

Then, enter the following directly below this line:

```
foreach ( T t in vals)
```

As you can see, the `foreach` loop here is going to operate. The `T` object will be a different data type, depending on how we choose to make the object. The `t` variable, of course, is each specific value inside the `vals` array.

Next, you will enter the following between a set of curly braces beneath the preceding line:

```
str += $"<br>Value={t}";
```

Remember, we use the `+=` operator to accumulate and `<br>` to push down to the next line. To get the value, of course, we will put in the `t` variable.

At the end, you want to return this, so you will type the following beneath the closed curly brace under the preceding line:

```
return str;
```

That's it. The final version of the `GenericsClass.cs` file for this chapter, including comments, is shown in the following code block:

```
//<T> means this class can operate on many different data types
public class GenericsClass<T>
{
    //generic array instance variable
    private T[] vals;//array of T inputs
    public GenericsClass(T[] input)
    {
        //set value of instance variable
        vals = input;
    }
    public string DisplayValues()
    {
        string str = null;//create string to build up display
        foreach(T t in vals)
        {
            //actually accumulate stuff to be displayed
            str += $"<br>Value={t}";
        }
    //return string of outputs to calling code
    return str;
    }
}
```

Notice that we have a single block of code; this will now operate on integers, doubles, and so on.

Adding a button to Default.aspx

Now, let's take a look at `Default.aspx`. The only thing we really need to do at this time is to add a `Button` control. For this, go to **Toolbox** and grab a `Button` control from there. Drag and drop it below the line beginning with `<form id=...` (you can delete the `<div>` lines, as we won't be needing them). Change the text on the `Button` control to, for example, `Display Values`. Your complete `Default.aspx` file should look like the one shown in *Figure 1.1.2*:

```
 1 <%@ Page Language="C#" AutoEventWireup="true" CodeFile="Default.aspx.cs" Inherits="_Default" %>
 2
 3 <!DOCTYPE html>
 4
 5 <html xmlns="http://www.w3.org/1999/xhtml">
 6 <head runat="server">
 7     <title>Our First Page</title>
 8 </head>
 9 <body>
10     <form id="form1" runat="server">
11         <asp:Button ID="Button1" runat="server" Text="Display Values" /><br />
12
13         <asp:Label ID="sampLabel" runat="server"></asp:Label>
14
15
16     </form>
17 </body>
18 </html>
19
```

Figure 1.1.2: The complete HTML for this project

Now, go to the **Design** view. Our very simple interface is shown in *Figure 1.1.3*:

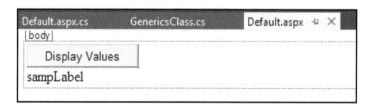

Figure 1.1.3: Our very simple interface in the Design view

Initializing a collection of integers to their array and displaying the results

Now, double-click on the `Display Values` button and go into `Default.aspx.cs`. Delete the `Page_Load` block. Next, between the set of curly braces beneath the line beginning with `protected void Button1_Click...`, enter the following:

```
GenericsClass<int> ints = new GenericsClass<int>(new int[] { 1, 2, 3, 4, 5
});
```

You can see in this line that we are basically initializing a collection of integers to their array.

Now, you can display this. So, for example, you can enter the following below this line:

```
sampLabel.Text += ints.DisplayValues();
```

Notice that the `GenericsClass` which we have constructed is operating in integers, but it can operate equally well on any other data type.

Changing the data types in our generics class

Now, to make the code efficiency more obvious, take both of the preceding lines, copy them (*Ctrl* + *C*) and paste them (*Ctrl* + *V*) beneath these and just change it to double, as follows:

```
GenericsClass<double> dubs = new GenericsClass<double>(new double[] {1, 2,
3, 4, 5});
sampLabel.Text = ints.DisplayValues();
```

We'll call this one `dubs` and change the name here to double: it's the same code, the same class, and the same generic class that you can operate on the doubles. Again, to emphasize this one more time, and to see that flexibility and code reuse is really the purpose here; that is, the ability to reuse code, we'll now take both of these new lines, copy and paste them below once more, and just change `double` to `decimal`, as follows:

```
GenericsClass<decimal> decs = new GenericsClass<decimal>(new decimal[] { 1,
2, 3, 4, 5 });
sampLabel.Text = ints.DisplayValues();
```

Let's call this one `decs`. Now, of course, if you want to make things a little more interesting, you can throw in some decimals:

```
GenericsClass<double> dubs = new GenericsClass<double>(new double[] { 1.0,
-2.3, 3, 4, 5 });
sampLabel.Text = ints.DisplayValues();
GenericsClass<decimal> decs = new GenericsClass<decimal>(new decimal[] { 1,
2.0M, 3, 4, 5.79M });
sampLabel.Text = ints.DisplayValues();
```

With decimals, just make sure that you put the M suffix in there, because you need the M suffix at the end to indicate that it's a decimal.

Running the program

Now, let's take a look. When you run this code and click on the **Display Values** button, your screen will look like the one shown in *Figure 1.1.4*:

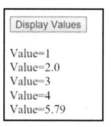

Figure 1.1.4: The initial run of our code

Accumulating the input

Now, we will accumulate the input. So, in the following `sampLabel.Text` lines, we change the = sign to +=, as shown here:

```
GenericsClass<double> dubs = new GenericsClass<double>(new double[] { 1.0,
-2.3, 3, 4, 5 });
sampLabel.Text += ints.DisplayValues();
GenericsClass<decimal> decs = new GenericsClass<decimal>(new decimal[] { 1,
2.0M, 3, 4, 5.79M });
sampLabel.Text += ints.DisplayValues();
```

Let's run it one more time. Click on the **Display Values** button and your screen will now look like the one shown in *Figure 1.1.5*:

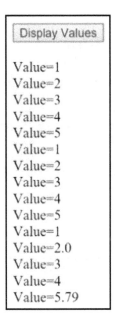

Figure 1.1.5: The input is now being accumulated, and the values are showing as expected

The program is now working as expected.

So, the big idea of generics at this point is that you can define a generic class. This class can operate equally well on many different data types. For example, you can make a generic class that operates on integers as well as on doubles and decimals.

This step isn't strictly required, but here's a little bit of additional insight. If you want to, you can set a breakpoint as follows. Select the line with the open curly brace under the line beginning with `protected void Button1_Click`.... Now, go to **Debug | Step Into** (*F11*) and click on **Display Values**.

Now, we will go through it. So, to first step into it, hover your mouse over the T object in the following line in `Generics Class.cs`:

```
public GenericsClass(T[] input)
```

Here, T is essentially like a parameter, so it does have a certain value, which is expressed in the `vals = input;` line. The first time, T is used for integers. This is how you can step through this code. At the bottom of the screen, the values inside the array are displayed, as shown in *Figure 1.1.6*:

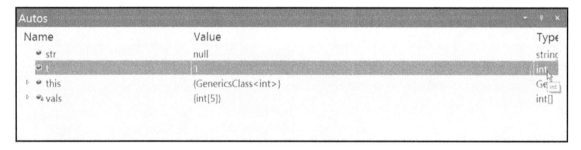

Figure 1.1.6: The values inside the array

The t variable, as you can see in *Figure 1.1.7*, is an integer, and this is how it operates:

Figure 1.1.7: The t is an integer

Notice also in the screenshot that it's a generics class with an `<int>` datatype.

The T object in the `foreach(T t in vals)` line right now represents an integer, and so on for the other data types. So, flexibility of code and reuse of code means that you will write less code. If not for generics, you would have to create individual classes to handle each different data type.

Chapter review

For review, the complete version of the `Default.aspx.cs` file for this chapter, including comments, is shown in the following code block:

```
//using is a directive
//System is a name space
//name space is a collection of features that our needs to run
using System;
//public means accessible anywhere
//partial means this class is split over multiple files
//class is a keyword and think of it as the outermost level of grouping
//:System.Web.UI.Page means our page inherits the features of a Page
public partial class _Default : System.Web.UI.Page
{
    protected void Button1_Click(object sender, EventArgs e)
    {
        //in each case below, GenericsClass<...> works equally well with
        //integers, doubles and decimals, among others
        GenericsClass<int> ints = new GenericsClass<int>(new int[] { 1, 2,
3, 4, 5 });
        sampLabel.Text = ints.DisplayValues();
        GenericsClass<double> dubs = new GenericsClass&lt;double>(new
double[] { 1.0, -2.3, 3, 4, 5 });
        sampLabel.Text += ints.DisplayValues();
        GenericsClass<decimal> decs = new GenericsClass<decimal>(new
decimal[] { 1, 2.0M, 3, 4, 5.79M });
        sampLabel.Text += decs.DisplayValues();
    }
}
```

Summary

In this chapter, you learned about the basics of making a simple generic class, so that one class can operate on many different data types. A great benefit of generics is flexibility. You created a simple generics class that worked with different data types, made generic parameters, initialized a collection of integers to their array and displayed the results, and then changed the data types in the generics class to doubles and decimals.

In the next chapter, you will learn about generic methods, or methods that can operate on different data types. You will also learn about constraining a method in terms of the data types that it can operate on, so we'll add a concept called constraints.

2
Creating a Generic Method

In this chapter, you'll learn about generic methods, which are methods that can operate on different data types. You will also learn about constraining a method in terms of the data types that it can operate on, so we'll add a concept called *constraints*.

Creating a button to exchange and then comparing two values

Open up a project and click on the **<html>** tab. The only thing to put in there is a button. This time, we will not read any values from the user just to save time. So, go to **Toolbox** and grab a `Button` control. Drag and drop it below the line beginning with `<form id=...` (you can delete the `<div>` lines, as we won't be needing them). Change the text on the button to say `Exchange And Compare`. So, this will exchange two values and then compare them. Your complete `Default.aspx` file should look like the one shown in *Figure 2.2.1*:

```
1 <%@ Page Language="C#" AutoEventWireup="true" CodeFile="Default.aspx.cs" Inherits="_Default" %>
2
3 <!DOCTYPE html>
4
5 <html xmlns="http://www.w3.org/1999/xhtml">
6 <head runat="server">
7     <title>Our First Page</title>
8 </head>
9 <body>
10     <form id="form1" runat="server">
11         <asp:Button ID="Button1" runat="server" Text="Exchange And Compare" /><br />
12         <asp:Label ID="Label1" runat="server" Text=""></asp:Label>
13
14     </form>
15 </body>
16 </html>
17
```

Figure 2.2.1: The complete HTML file for this chapter

Writing a swap function

A *swap* function is a common thing to write: a function that swaps two values. To do this, go to **Solution Explorer**, right-click on the name of the website, select **Add**, and then click on **Class**. Name the class GenMethods to keep it simple, and then click on **OK**. When the Visual Studio message comes up, click on **Yes**.

When the GenMethods file comes up, the only thing that you should leave there is using System. We don't need the constructor for this class, so get rid of that. Then, within the body of GenMethods, define the following between the set of curly braces below the public class GenMethods line:

```
public static void Swap<T>(ref T x, ref T y)
```

This will act at the class level: you don't have to make an object of the GenMethods type. In a sense, the only thing that is new here is the fact that this is a Swap<T> function, which means that it can act on several different data types equally well. Now, also remember that the ref keyword indicates that with the x and y parameters in this line, when you change the values inside the method, those changed values are also accessible inside the calling code. Keep that in mind.

Before going ahead, let's label this by entering the following comment above this line:

```
//method can operate on multiple data types
```

This basically means that the method can operate on multiple data types equally.

Now, between the set of curly braces beneath the preceding line, enter the following to swap the values:

```
T temp = x;
```

Here, you're taking the value of x and assigning it to a temporary one. Then, in the next stage, you can take x and assign y to it and then you can take y and assign temp to it, as follows:

```
x = y;
y = temp;
```

Let's add the following comments before proceeding:

```
T temp = x;
//save x
x = y;
//assign y to x
y = temp;
//assign original value of x back to y
```

Here, the first line means overwrite the value of x with the value of y, and then you assign y to x. In the last stage, you assign `temp`, which is the original value of x, back to y. This represents the switching of the values.

Comparing values using the CompareTo method

Now, let's do one more method. This one will be a little more sophisticated. It will be called `Compare`, and it will operate on different data types. So, enter the following beneath the closed curly brace at the end of the preceding lines:

```
public static string Compare<T>(T x, T y) where T : IComparable
```

Introducing constraints

To compare values, you want to use the `CompareTo` method. It can be used if you have `where T : IComparable`. This is a new construct there. It's a *constraint*. The `Compare` method works, but it only does so if the data type on which it is operating has `IComparable` implemented on it. In other words, it makes sense to compare the values.

Completing the GenMethods class

For the next stage, you can say the following. Enter it within a set of curly braces below this line:

```
if(x.CompareTo(y) < 0)
```

Now, why do we write this? We write this because if you right-click on the `CompareTo` method and select **Go To Definition** in the drop-down menu (*F12*), you can see that it's defined inside the `IComparable` interface. If you expand that and look at what it returns, it says: **Values Meaning Less than zero This instance precedes obj in the sort order.**, as shown in *Figure 2.2.2*:

```
// Returns:
//      A value that indicates the relative order of the objects being compared. The
//      return value has these meanings: Value Meaning Less than zero This instance precedes
//      obj in the sort order. Zero This instance occurs in the same position in the
//      sort order as obj. Greater than zero This instance follows obj in the sort order.
```

Figure 2.2.2: The definition of IComparable

In other words, in our context, this means that x and y are related in the following sense.

If the value returned by `CompareTo` is less than 0, then x is less than y.

Now, enter the following within a set of curly braces beneath the preceding line:

```
return $"<br>{x}<{y}";
```

In this line, you return and actually format a string, so that it's more than just a simple comparison. So, for example, you can say here x is less than y.

The other possibility is the reverse. Now, enter the following beneath the earlier closed curly brace:

```
else
{
    return $"<br>{x}>{y}";
}
```

If you want to know more about `CompareTo`, right-click on it and select **Go To Definition** in the drop-down menu (*F12*). As seen under **Returns** in *Figure 7.2.3*, it says: **Zero This instance occurs in the same position in a sort order as obj. Greater than zero This instance follows object in the sort order.**:

```
// Returns:
//      A value that indicates the relative order of the objects being compared. The
//      return value has these meanings: Value Meaning Less than zero This instance precedes
//      obj in the sort order. Zero This instance occurs in the same position in the
//      sort order as obj. Greater than zero This instance follows obj in the sort order.
```

Figure 2.2.3: The definition of CompareTo

In the if (x.CompareTo(y) < 0) line, this instance signifies the x variable and object denotes the y variable.

So, this is the basic GenMethods class. The final version of the GenMethods.cs file, including comments, is shown in the following code block:

```
using System;
public class GenMethods
{
    //method can operate on multiple data types
    public static void Swap<T>(ref T x, ref T y)
    {
        T temp = x; //save x
        x = y;//assign y to x
        y = temp;//assign original value of x back to y
    }
    //this function has a constraint, so it can operate on values
    //that can be compared
    public static string Compare<T>(T x, T y) where T :IComparable
    {
        //CompareTo returns < 0, =0,or >0, depending on the relationship
        //between x and y
        if(x.CompareTo(y)<0)
        {
            return $"<br>{x}<{y}";
        }
        else
        {
            return $"<br>{x}>{y}";
        }
    }
}
```

As you can see, the GenMethods class contains a couple of generic functions because it can operate on different data types, except for the second CompareTo method, which is a slightly more restricted version, meaning that a constraint is applied of the IComparable type.

Hardcoding the values

Now, back in Default.aspx, go to the **Design view** and double-click on the **Exchange and Compare** button. All we will do is to hardcode the values to save time. We don't have to read them from the user. Of course, you can, if you want to, by putting in two boxes and process that using double convert.

Now, in `Default.aspx.cs`, between a set of curly braces below the line beginning with `protected void Button1_Click...`, enter the following lines:

```
double x = 25, y = 34;
```

Then use `sampLabel.Text` to display the original values on this screen, first displaying the value of x and then displaying the value of y:

```
sampLabel.Text = $"x={x}, y={y}";
```

Next, to do the swapping of the values. Enter the following:

```
GenMethods.Swap<double>(ref x, ref y);
```

First, you enter the name of class and then the function, which is `Swap`. You will see that `<T>` can now be replaced with `<double>`, because we are swapping doubles. Then, you'll put in `ref x` and `ref y`.

Because we are using `ref`, the values of x and y have to be initialized and further now we can display them again, but swapped, as shown here:

```
sampLabel.Text += $"<br>x={x}, y={y}";
```

Running the program

Let's take a look at the effects and see if this is working as expected. So, give it a go in your browser. Click on the **Exchange and Compare** button. The results are shown in *Figure 2.2.4*:

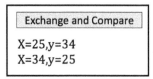

Figure 2.2.4: Results of the initial program run

As you can see, **x** is 25 and **y** is 34. Then, after you click on **Exchange and Compare**, x is 34 and **y** is 25. So, this is working as expected.

Modifying the program for an additional type of comparison

Now, go back to `Default.aspx` and, in the next stage, in the **Design** view, we will also compare those values. For this, double-click on the **Exchange and Compare** button again and add the following beneath the last line we entered:

```
sampLabel.Text += GenMethods.Compare<double>(x, y);
```

Remember that the way we designed `Compare`, it returns a string that returns one of the two values, depending on the specifics. So, in this line we will compare `double`; so you put that in there and then the two values will be x, y.

Let's give it a shot in your browser. Click on the **Exchange and Compare** button once again. The new results are shown in *Figure 2.2.5*:

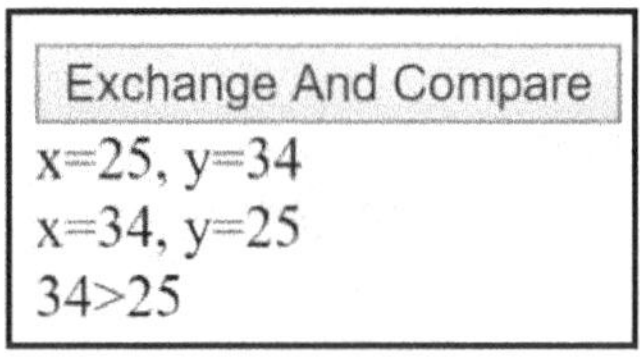

Exchange And Compare
x=25, y=34
x=34, y=25
34>25

Figure 2.2.5: Results of the modified program run

Now, **x** is 25 and **y** is 34. When you exchange the values, **x** is 34 and **y** is 25. Further, 34 is certainly more than 25. It looks really nice and professional.

Modifying the program for different data types

The nice thing now is this: imagine you want to redo this; you can just type `int` as an example and change the data type to an integer or decimal type and the methods. The code that we wrote in this chapter operates equally well on these things:

```
int x = 25, y = 34;
sampLabel.Text = $"x={x}, y={y}";
GenMethods.Swap<int> (ref x, ref y);
sampLabel.Text += $"<br>x={x}, y={y}";
sampLabel.Text += GenMethods.Compare<int>(x, y);
```

The only thing is, of course, if you right-click on int and select **Go To Definition** in the drop-down menu (*F12*), you'll see that it says public struct Int32 and it implements IComparable:

```
12    ...public struct Int32 : IComparable, IFormattable, IConvertible, IComparable<Int32>, IEquatable<Int32>
```

Figure 2.2.6: Definition for public struct Int32

This will work due to the fact that our function has a constraint where it says where T should be comparable, as shown here:

```
public static string Compare<T>(T x, T y) where T : IComparable
```

These are the basics.

Chapter review

For review, the complete version of the Default.aspx.cs file for this chapter, including comments, is shown in the following code block:

```
//using is a directive
//System is a name space
//name space is a collection of features that our needs to run
using System;
//public means accessible anywhere
//partial means this class is split over multiple files
//class is a keyword and think of it as the outermost level of grouping
//:System.Web.UI.Page means our page inherits the features of a Page
public partial class _Default : System.Web.UI.Page
{
    protected void Button1_Click(object sender, EventArgs e)
    {
        int x = 25, y = 34;//declare and set two variables
        sampLabel.Text = $"x={x}, y={y}";//display variables
        GenMethods.Swap (ref x, ref y);//swap values
        sampLabel.Text += $"<br>x={x}, y={y}";//display swapped values
        sampLabel.Text += GenMethods.Compare (x, y);
    }
}
```

Summary

In this chapter, you learned about generic methods, which are methods that can operate on different data types. You also learned about constraining a method in terms of the data types that it can operate on, a concept called *constraints*. You created a GenMethods class, wrote a Swap function, compared values using the CompareTo method, learned about constraints, and modified the program to perform additional types of comparisons and to work with different data types.

In the next chapter, you will learn about up casting, down casting, and then how to implement a generic interface and how that exactly helps us.

3
Implementing a Generic Interface to Accomplish Sorting

In this chapter, you'll learn upcasting and downcasting and then how to implement a generic interface and how exactly that helps us.

Imagine that you have a list of objects, which you have made of your own type, and you want to sort them. You'll need to figure out just how you can sort these objects. This comes from implementing IComparable, a generic interface that can act on different data types.

Adding a button to sort and display results

Open up a project and click on the **<html>** tab. Once again, the only thing that you need to put in there is a button. For this, go to **Toolbox** and grab a Button control. Drag and drop it below the line beginning with <form id=... and change the text on the button to say Sort and Show. Now, put a <br> tag in there at the end of the line and keep the label as usual:

```
<asp:Button ID="Button1" runat="server" Text="Sort And Show"/><br />
```

Now, go to the **Design** view, where you should see only the **Sort and Show** button as shown in *Figure 3.3.1*.

Figure 3.3.1: Adding a button

Creating a generics interface class

Next, go to **Solution Explorer**. Right-click on the name of the website, select **Add**, and then click on **Class**. Name the class GenInterface and then click on **OK**. When the Visual Studio message comes up, click on **Yes**. Remember, this is just an example.

The code for the GenInterface class is really complex. I'll create it now line-by-line, explaining what I'm doing and why I'm doing it.

First, delete everything except using System; at the very top. Next, you'll make the class called Quad for a four-sided shape of some kind. Enter the following after using System:

```
public class Quad : IComparable<Quad>
```

This needs System so that we can use IComparable. If you right-click on it and select **Go To Definition** in the drop-down menu (*F12*), you can see the definition of this thing. You will see namespace System near the top, and the public intCompareTo (T other); function after the Returns definition, as shown in *Figure 3.3.2*:

```
namespace System
{
    ...public interface IComparable<in T>
    {
        //
        // Summary:
        //     Compares the current object with another object of the same type.
        //
        // Parameters:
        //   other:
        //     An object to compare with this object.
        //
        // Returns:
        //     A value that indicates the relative order of the objects being compared. The
        //     return value has the following meanings: Value Meaning Less than zero This object
        //     is less than the other parameter.Zero This object is equal to other. Greater
        //     than zero This object is greater than other.
        int CompareTo(T other);
    }
}
```

Figure 3.3.2: The definition of IComparable

Notice that it returns an integer. So, when we implement this interface, we have to keep that in mind. Now, close the definition window.

In our particular case, enter the following text below the open curly brace under the line beginning with `public class Quad...`:

```
private string name;
public Quad(string na)
```

Now, to set the value, enter the following between a set of curly braces beneath the preceding lines:

```
name = na;
```

After all, every quadrilateral shape, which is a square, rectangle, or rhombus, all have a name, don't they? So, it's a good idea to centralize the name feature in the `Quad class`.

Implementing the interface

Next, because IComparable has a function, right-click on it, select **Quick Actions**, and choose **Implement interface** from the popup. Now, we have to write code.

First, delete throw new NotImplementedException(). Now, we will implement the interface in a way that's sufficient to illustrate the point. For this, enter the following beneath the open curly brace under the public int CompareTo(Quad other) line:

```
if(this.name.CompareTo(other.name) <0)
```

Here, this means the current object, and the name of this object is compared to other.name, meaning the other object. Look at where it says (Quad other) in the line above this one; in other words, we're comparing two Quads. So, in the one on the left, this is the one on which the function is being invoked and the other Quad class is the one against which it's being compared. So, if this is less than 0, we will return a number such as -1, else it can return some other value, such as 1. Enter the following between a set of curly braces below this line:

```
{
    return -1;
}
else
{
    return 1;
}
```

We have just implemented CompareTo. Now, notice that the *this* is not necessary. You can remove it and it will still work. Remember, however, that name essentially means the current object under which CompareTo will be invoked. This is why I like to have the this keyword present, because it is more suggestive of what I want to know.

Basically, what this line is saying is that if the current object when compared to the other name is less than 0, then we return -1, which means that the current object will come before the next object in the list when you sort it. That's a simple interpretation.

Adding a virtual function

Now, in the next stage, we will add a virtual function called `Perimeter`. For this, enter the following beneath the closed curly brace:

```
public virtual string Perimeter()
```

Again, we'll centralize as much as we can. So, enter the following within a set of curly braces below this line:

```
return $"The perimeter of {name} is ";
```

The specific name can come from this line, because the `name` instance variable is declared above in `private string name`. However, the `Perimeter` will come from the derived classes.

So now, enter the following beneath the preceding closed curly brace:

```
public class Square : Quad
```

Adding refinements

Now we add class-specific refinements; for this, enter the following between a set of curly braces beneath the preceding line:

```
private double sideLength;
public Square(string n, double s) : base(n) {sideLength = s;}
```

Here, `string n` is the name and `doubles` is the side. Then, call the `base` class constructor with the name (n) and then enter `sideLength = s`. Remember, when you are calling the `base` class constructor, you're reusing code.

I've chosen to express this as a single line just to save space. Remember that, normally, it would look like this:

```
private double sideLength;
public Square(string n, double s) : base(n)
{
    sideLength = s;
}
```

Next, we have to implement an override version of `Perimeter`. So, enter the following beneath the preceding closed curly brace:

```
public override string Perimeter()
```

Now, we want to keep `return base.Perimeter()`, which appears automatically, because it provides the useful default functionality, `$"The perimeter of {name} is ";`, from the preceding return line: we don't want to keep typing that. What we do want to do is add a small refinement. So, add the following refinement to `return base.Perimeter()`:

```
return base.Perimeter() + 4 * sideLength;
```

This means four times the `sideLength` variable, because to find the perimeter of a square, you take four multiplied by the length of one side.

Refinement comes from the derived class generic functionality, which is equally applicable to all the classes you stick into a virtual method in the `base` class: you don't have to keep writing it.

Next, we can repeat this for our rectangle. So, copy the `public class Square : Quad` block (*Ctrl + C*) and then paste (*Ctrl +& V*) down below:

```
public class Rectangle : Quad
{
    private double sideOne, sideTwo;
    public Rectangle(string n, double s1, double s2) : base(n)
    {
        sideOne = s1; sideTwo = s2;
    }
    public override string Perimeter()
    {
        return base.Perimeter() + (2 * sideOne + 2 * sideTwo);
    }
}
```

Now, make the following changes:

1. Rename this block to `Rectangle`. This is also derived from `Quad`, so that's fine.
2. Change where it says `sideLength`; because a rectangle has two different side lengths, so change that to say `sideOne` and `sideTwo`.
3. Change `public Square` to `public Rectangle` as the name of the constructor. It calls the base class constructor with the name.
4. Then, initialize the other two, so now you'll say `double s1` and `double s2`.

5. Next, you have to initialize the fields, so say `sideOne = s1;` and `sideTwo = s2;`. That's it: they've been initialized.

6. Now again, override `Perimeter` inside the `Rectangle` class as shown earlier. Here, you specify the bit that applies to rectangles, so `(2 * sideOne + 2 * sideTwo)`. Make sure that you enclose this within parentheses, so that the calculation is done first and then it's combined together with `base.Perimeter` with the rest of it.

So, that's that class. For reference, the complete version of the `GenInterface` class, including comments, is shown in the following code block:

```
using System;
public class Quad:IComparable<Quad>//implement IComparable
{
    private string name;//instance field
    public Quad(string na)
    {
        name = na;//set value of instance field
    }
    //implement CompareTo to make list sortable
    //in this case, the items are sorted by name
    public int CompareTo(Quad other)
    {
        if(this.name.CompareTo(other.name) < 0)
        {
            return -1;
        }
        else
        {
            return 1;
        }
    }//put default code inside Perimeter
    public virtual string Perimeter()
    {
        return $"The perimeter of {name} is ";
    }
}
public class Square: Quad
{
    private double sideLength;
    public Square(string n, double s):base(n)
    {
        sideLength = s;
    }
    //override Perimeter, calling the base portion
    //and then adding refinement with 4*sideLength
```

```
    public override string Perimeter()
    {
        return base.Perimeter() + 4 * sideLength;
    }
}
public class Rectangle: Quad
{
    private double sideOne, sideTwo;
    public Rectangle(string n, double s1, double s2) : base(n)
    {
        sideOne = s1; sideTwo = s2;
    }
    //override Perimeter, calling the base portion
    //and then adding refinement with 2sideOne+2sideTwo
    public override string Perimeter()
    {
        return base.Perimeter() + (2 * sideOne + 2 * sideTwo);
    }
}
```

Entering the reference code

Now, I'll do my reference code. This code is mechanical. There's a lot of it, but it's mechanical. Remember, the big idea here is that IComparable is being implemented using the CompareTo method inside the Quad class, which means that now when we stick different shapes into a list of quads, we will be able to sort them in some fashion. So, now our names will be sorted. In our case, we'll be sorting them by name.

Now go to Default.aspx, and enter the **Design** view. Double-click on the **Sort and Show** button. This takes us into Default.aspx.cs. Delete the Page_Load block.

Next, between the set of curly braces under the line beginning with protected void Button1_Click..., the first thing we'll do is to put a Quad on the left-hand side and we'll call it sqr:

```
Quad sqr = new Square("Square", 4);
```

Upcasting

Notice that I've written `new Square`. This is *upcasting*. Here, this involves converting the object on the right-hand side, because it's derived from its `Quad`. On the left-hand side, you can make a `Quad` namespace and put an object that is of a derived type on the right side; so, we'll call this one `Square` and then enter a side length of `4`.

Next, enter the following directly below this line:

```
Quad rect = new Rectangle("Rectangle", 2, 5);
```

Again, we put a `Quad` namespace on the left-hand side, and this time we called it `rect`. We give it the name `Rectangle`, and then we put in two sides of lengths 2 and 5.

Now, you can store this in a list, for example, which you can sort. Imagine if you had many of these, you would need a way to sort this information. So now, go to the top of this file, and enter the following beneath `using System`:

```
using System.Collections.Generic;
```

Next, under the `Quad rect` ... line, enter the following:

```
List<Quad> lst = new List<Quad>(new Quad[] { sqr, rect, rect2, sqr1 });
```

We'll call this list `new List<Quad>`, and to initialize a list you can always use an array. To do this, type `new Quad` and then initialize it with `sqr` and `rect`. This is how you can always initialize a list within an array.

Then, to sort the list, enter the following directly below this line:

```
lst.Sort();
```

So, this makes sense now. It doesn't give an error. Imagine if you didn't have `IComparable<Quad>` at the top of the `GenInterface` class. This sort would not work. If you cut `IComparable<Quad>`, and then take the `CompareTo` method out, you will have problems. So, for our purposes, we now have a way of sorting these `Quads` classes.

For the last stage, start by entering the following below the `Sort` line:

```
if(lst[0] is Square)
```

So, `is` is a new keyword. You can use it to check whether something is of a certain type.

Downcasting

Now, we will talk about *downcasting*, which means going from, for example, a parent type to a child type. Enter the following between a set of curly braces below this line:

```
sampLabel.Text += ((Square)lst[0]).Perimeter();
```

Now, beneath the closed curly brace after the preceding line, enter the following:

```
else if(lst[0] is Rectangle)
```

Then, you can call the following code; so, copy the `sampLabel.Text...` line and paste it between a set of curly braces:

```
sampLabel.Text += ((Rectangle)lst[0]).Perimeter();
```

Be sure to change `Square` to `Rectangle`, so that it gets cast down to a rectangle, and then the `Perimeter` function on the rectangle will be called. When you hover your mouse over `Perimeter` in the preceding two lines, the popups show `string Square.Perimeter()` and `string Square.Perimeter()`, respectively. If you removed `(Rectangle)` from the preceding line and hovered your mouse over `Perimeter`, the popup will show `string Quad.Perimeter()`. Do you understand? This is why I have the cast: because it changes the way the functions are recognized.

This is downcasting from a parent to a child class. So, when we talk about bulk actions, you cannot cast to a parent class, perform a bulk action like a sort, or if you want to add refinements called child classes and child class objects, then you can downcast.

Running the program

Now, let's take a look. Open the program in your browser and click on the **Sort And Show** button. The results are shown in *Figure 3.3.3*:

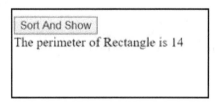

Figure 3.3.3: The results of running the program

This is indeed the perimeter of the rectangle.

These are the basics of upcasting, downcasting, and implementing a generic interface such as IComparable. This is really complex code, but I hope you've learned a lot.

Chapter review

For review, the complete version of the Default.aspx.cs file for this chapter, including comments, is shown in the following code block:

```
//using is a directive
//System is a name space
//name space is a collection of features that our needs to run
using System;
using System.Collections.Generic;
//public means accessible anywhere
//partial means this class is split over multiple files
//class is a keyword and think of it as the outermost level of grouping
//:System.Web.UI.Page means our page inherits the features of a Page
public partial class _Default : System.Web.UI.Page
{
    protected void Button1_Click(object sender, EventArgs e)
    {
        sampLabel.Text = "";//clear label every time
        Quad sqr = new Square("John",4);//make a square
        Quad rect = new Rectangle("Bob", 2, 5);//make a rectangle
        Quad rect2 = new Rectangle("Jerry", 4, 5);//make another rectangle
        //stick all these shapes into a list of quads
        List<Quad> lst = new List<Quad>(new Quad[] { sqr, rect,rect2});
        lst.Sort();//sort the list
        if(lst[0] is Square) //if it's asquare
        {
            //down cast to a square, and call Perimeter on it
            sampLabel.Text += ((Square)lst[0]).Perimeter();
        }
        else if(lst[0] is Rectangle)
        {
            //if it's a rectangle, down cost to a rectangle,
            //and call Perimeter
            sampLabel.Text += ((Rectangle)lst[0]).Perimeter();
        }
    }
}
```

Summary

In this chapter, you learned upcasting, downcasting, and then how to implement a generic interface and how that exactly helps us. You created a Generics Interface class and a Quad class, implemented an interface, added a virtual `Perimeter` function, added refinements to the code, and entered a lot of mechanical reference code.

In the next chapter, you will learn about generic delegates.

4

Making Delegates More Flexible with Generics

In this chapter, you'll learn about generic delegates. Remember, as in the previous lessons, the fundamental benefit is that generics allow you to create flexible code that can handle a variety of data types with ease. If there were no generics, you'd have to create a lot more code.

Adding a summarize button to the HTML

Bring up a project. In the basic HTML, delete the `<div>` lines, as you won't need them. Now, let's add a button. The only thing the button will do is to summarize some information for us.

Go to **Toolbox** and grab a `Button` control. Drag and drop it below the line beginning with `<form id=...`, and change the text on the button to say `Summarize`. Now, close this with a `<br>` tag and keep the `Label` control as usual.

Now, go to `Default.aspx`, and enter the **Design** view. You'll see one button for the interface, which says **Summarize** and looks like *Figure 4.4.1*:

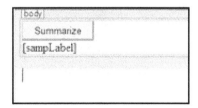

Figure 4.4.1: The simple interface for this project

Now, double-click on the **Summarize** button. This takes us into `Default.aspx.cs`. Delete the `Page_Load` block. Your initial code screen for this project should look like *Figure 4.4.2*:

```
1 //using is a directive
2 //System is a name space
3 //name space is a collection of features that our needs to run
4 using System;
5 //public means accessible anywhere
6 //partial means this class is split over multiple files
7 //class is a keyword and think of it as the outermost level of grouping
8 //:System.Web.UI.Page means our page inherits the features of a Page
9
10 public partial class _Default : System.Web.UI.Page
11 {
12     protected void Button1_Click(object sender, EventArgs e)
13     {
14
15     }
16 }
```

Figure 4.4.2: The initial Default.aspx.cs code for this project

Constructing a delegate

First, in order to make the delegate, above the line beginning with `public partial class...`, enter the following:

```
public delegate void Summarize<T>(T x, T y);
```

Here, `public` means accessible anywhere, `delegate` is a keyword, and `void` doesn't return a value. The delegate name is `Summarize`, and it can act on different data types because `T` is present and not integer, double, or something like that. `T` is a generic.

Now remember, delegates serve essentially as function wrappers. Correct? You use them to point to multiple functions, so you can cascade function calls, for example. The same principle holds here. So, for example, to make use of this, enter the following between a set of curly braces under the line beginning with `protected void Button1_Click...`:

```
Summarize<double> s =
```

Assigning functions to represent the delegate

For the right-hand side, we first need to start assigning the functions that it represents. To do this, we can say the following, for example, below the closed curly brace after this line:

```
public void FindSum(double x, double y)
```

Imagine that the first thing you'll do is to find the sum of two values. So, you say, for example, `Find Sum` and then `double x` and `double y`.

Then, you can update the labels; so, enter the following between a set of curly braces below this line:

```
sampLabel.Text = $"<br>{x}+{y}={x + y}";
```

Now, you can assign `FindSum` to `<int>` in the preceding line. You can set this equal, as follows:

```
Summarize<double> s = FindSum;
```

Of course, there are many other operations that you can perform. So, let's take this code: this basic function that adds, and define some other operations. Copy (*Ctrl + C*) these two lines and paste (*Ctrl + V*) them down below. This time, change `FindSum` to `FindRatio` and basically follow the same plan. We'll apply a `+=` operator to make sure that it's appending. Then, to make a new line, put a `<br>` tag in there and, instead of `x + y`, change these to `x / y`. Of course, here you'd have to ensure that `y` is not `0`. We can figure that out:

```
public void FindRatio(decimal x, decimal y)
{
    sampLabel.Text += $"<br>{x}/{y}={x / y}";
}
```

Let's do one more. So again, copy these two lines and paste them down below. This time, change `FindRatio` to `FindProduct`, which is the result of multiplying two values, and change `x / y` to `x * y`.

```
public void FindProduct(decimal x, decimal y)
{
    sampLabel.Text += $"<br>{x}*{y}={x * y}";
}
```

Reminder: If it's brown (Windows) or orange (Mac) it shows on the screen exactly as it is.

Always remember to put in the `<br>` tags so that stuff gets pushed down to the next line.

Calling the delegate

Now, we have to stack up these calls; so, enter the following beneath the `Summarize<double> s = FindSum;` line:

```
s += FindRatio;
s += FindProduct;
```

Note that you put the next function name, `FindRatio`, and then the next line will be `FindProduct`.

Then, of course, to call it, enter the following on the very next line:

```
s(4, 5);
```

This is how you would invoke that delegate: you will call it, specify the name, and then pass in those values of 4 and 5.

The complete version of the `Default.aspx.cs` file for the `double` data type, including comments, is shown in the following code block:

```
//using is a directive
//System is a name space
//name space is a collection of features that our needs to run
using System;
//public means accessible anywhere
//partial means this class is split over multiple files
//class is a keyword and think of it as the outermost level of grouping
//:System.Web.UI.Page means our page inherits the features of a Page
public delegate void Summarize<T>(T x, T y);//declare generic delegate
public partial class _Default : System.Web.UI.Page
{
    protected void Button1_Click(object sender, EventArgs e)
    {
        Summarize<decimal> s = FindSum;//assign FindSum to the delegate
        s += FindRatio;//assign FindRatio to the delegate
        s += FindProduct;//assign FindProduct to the delegate
        s(4, 5);//invoke the delegate, causing the chain of functions to be
```

```
executed
    }
    public void FindSum(decimal x, decimal y)
    {
        sampLabel.Text = $"<br>{x}+{y}={x + y}";
    }
    public void FindRatio(decimal x, decimal y)
    {
        sampLabel.Text += $"<br>{x}/{y}={x / y}";
    }
    public void FindProduct(decimal x, decimal y)
    {
        sampLabel.Text += $"<br>{x}*{y}={x * y}";
    }
}
```

Running the program

Now, let's take a look at the effects. For this, launch the program in your browser. Click on the **Summarize** button. The results are shown in *Figure 4.4.3*:

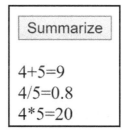

Figure 4.4.3: The results of running our program for this project

As you can see, **4+5=9, 4/5=0.8**, and **4*5=20**. So, it's working as expected. The `public delegate void Summarize<T>(T x, T y);` line is a single, generic delegate and, because it has `T` there and not a fixed data type such as integer or double, it can operate on different data types.

Now, if you take your `Default.aspx.cs` page and search for all occurrences of `double` and replace them with `int`, seven occurrences will be replaced. If you run the code again, you'll see that it works equally well. Just to illustrate the point further, replace `int` with `decimal` and again seven occurrences are replaced. Now, it will be operating in decimal types and, if you click on the **Summarize** button once more, you'll see that it works equally well.

So, there you have a generic delegate. Remember, with a single button click, you can basically invoke a whole list of functions by chaining them together through the s delegate, which is of the Summarize type, which is generic so that it can operate on different data types equally well.

Summary

In this chapter, you learned about generic delegates. You constructed a delegate, assigned functions to represent the delegate, and called the delegate.

In the next chapter, you will learn about generic dictionaries.

5
Creating and Using Generic Dictionaries

In this chapter, you'll learn about generic dictionaries. Dictionaries are used to store *key-value pairs*.

Adding a show button to the HTML

Bring up Visual Studio. We need to place a button inside **<html>**; so, go to **Toolbox** and grab a `Button` control. Drag and drop it below the line beginning with `<form id=....` Change the text on the button to say `Show`. You can delete the `<div>` lines, as you don't need them.

Starting a process from a web page

What we will do in this chapter is to learn how to open, for example, Notepad and then explore directly from a page. For this, go to `Default.aspx`, and enter the **Design** view. Double-click on the **Show** button. This takes us into `Default.aspx.cs`.

Delete the `Page_Load` block, so that it looks like the screen shown in *Figure 5.5.1*:

```
 1 //using is a directive
 2 //System is a name space
 3 //name space is a collection of features that our needs to run
 4 using System;
 5
 6
 7
 8
 9 public partial class _Default : System.Web.UI.Page
10 {
11     protected void Button1_Click(object sender, EventArgs e)
12     {
13
14     }
15 }
16
```

Figure 5.5.1: The initial Default.aspx.cs code for this project

First, below the `using System` line, enter the following:

```
using System.Collections.Generic;
```

You add this line because we are dealing with dictionaries. Then, add one more line below this:

```
using System.Diagnostics;
```

You will see shortly why this line is needed. This is how you can start a process. A *process*, for example, refers to Notepad.

Now, between the set of curly braces beneath the line beginning with `protected void Button1_Click...`, enter the following:

```
Dictionary<string, string> filePrograms = new Dictionary<string, string>();
```

Hover your mouse over `Dictionary` and look at the pop-up tip, as shown in *Figure 5.5.2*. Do you see where it says **TKey**? This indicates the type of key, and **TValue** specifies the type of value. In our case, both will be of the `string` type:

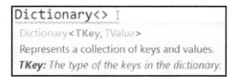

Figure 5.5.2: Pop-up tip for Dictionary

Note that we give the dictionary a name such as `filePrograms`. Next, to make memory for it, enter `new Dictionary<string, string>` to indicate the type of key and the type of value and close this with a semicolon.

In the next stage, we will fill this dictionary. So, enter the following directly below this line:

```
filePrograms.Add("notepad.exe", @"c:\data\samplefile.txt");
```

Making a verbatim string

In the preceding line, you need to specify the key-value pairs within the parentheses. The key is `notepad.exe`. If you try to put a path such as `c:\data\samplefile.txt` directly into your code, it doesn't work. You see how it gets underlined red? The popup says **Represents text as a series of Unicode characters**. These things don't work. So, to fix this, you put the @ (at) symbol in front of it. Now, you have a *verbatim string*.

With the old approach, this is how you handled this: `c:\\data\\samplefile.txt`. This is called *character escaping*. If you try this with the preceding line, notice that the red underline goes away because `c:\` already means something. So, to escape the usual meaning, you add the second backslash. This is the old way, though. The new way for this situation is to use a verbatim, string so that it's interpreted exactly as it appears.

In this context here, Notepad is the key and the value is the `samplefile.txt` file.

Next, enter the following line directly beneath the preceding one:

```
filePrograms.Add("iexplore.exe", "http://www.bing.com");
```

So, Internet Explorer will open the `http://www.bing.com` page. You see?

Iterating over key-value pairs

Now, imagine that we want to iterate over these keys, because we potentially have many of them. One way to do this is as follows:

```
foreach(KeyValuePair<string, string> kvp in filePrograms)
```

You can iterate over key-value pairs like this. Next, enter the following between a set of curly braces beneath the preceding line:

```
Process.Start(kvp.Key, kvp.Value);
```

Here, after `Process.start`, you display the key and the values. So, you can say `kvp.key`, which is a property of the key-value pair and `kvp.value` is a property of the key-value pair as well.

In a realistic application, where a program could be missing or something else could happen, it would be better to put this in a `TryCatch` block and so on, but for our purposes, this is sufficient and it keeps it short.

If you want, you can also iterate over individual keys and values and so on. So, as another example, you can do something like the following beneath the closed curly brace under the preceding line:

```
foreach(string key in filePrograms.Keys)
```

To get the individual keys, you type the name of the dictionary and then the name of the keys collection, `Keys`, which appears in the popup.

This is how you can access just the keys. If you want to display them, you definitely can; to do this, enter the following between a set of curly braces under this line:

```
sampLabel.Txt += $"<br>{key}";
```

To show the key, you type `{key}`. Remember to insert the `<br>` tag, the `+=` operator to append, the `$` symbol, and close with a semicolon.

Making a directory and creating a file from Command Prompt

Now, you want to make sure that you have the `samplefile.txt` file. So, to do that in Windows, type `cmd`, which is short for **Command Prompt**, and open that. At the `C:\>` prompt, start by typing `cd..` to go up one level and then `cd..` again to go up another level. Then enter `cd data` to change to the data directory. The system responds that this path does not exist, as you can see in *Figure 5.5.3*; so, we'll have to create the path and make the file:

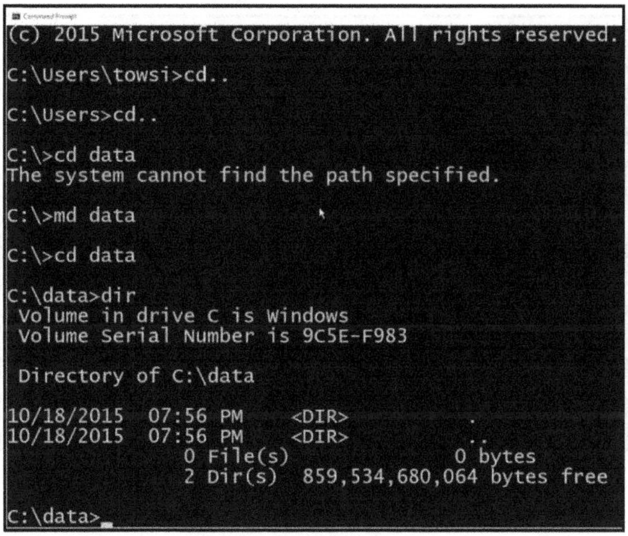

```
(c) 2015 Microsoft Corporation. All rights reserved.

C:\Users\towsi>cd..

C:\Users>cd..

C:\>cd data
The system cannot find the path specified.

C:\>md data

C:\>cd data

C:\data>dir
 Volume in drive C is Windows
 Volume Serial Number is 9C5E-F983

 Directory of C:\data

10/18/2015  07:56 PM    <DIR>          .
10/18/2015  07:56 PM    <DIR>          ..
               0 File(s)              0 bytes
               2 Dir(s)  859,534,680,064 bytes free

C:\data>
```

Figure 5.5.3: The system indicates that the path c:\>data does not exist

To create the path, type the following at command prompt:

    C:\>**md data**

Then, enter the following to change into that directory:

    C:\>**cd data**

Next, type the following to show you the list of files in the directory:

`C:\data\dir`

As you can see in the *Figure 5.5.3*, there is nothing inside the directory: it's new, we just created it. So, to open a file in Notepad, type the following at the prompt:

`C:\data\notepad.exe samplefile.txt`

This makes the file. When the screen prompt asks if you want to create a new file, click on the **Yes** button. This will open a blank Notepad file. Enter some text, as shown in *Figure 5.5.4*:

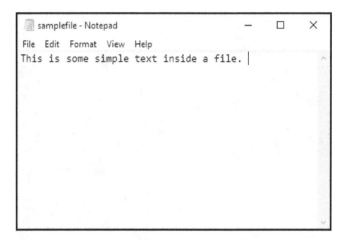

Figure 5.5.4: Enter some text in the new Notepad file you created

Make sure that you save it in the C:\data directory (*Ctrl + S*) and then you can close it.

Now, take a look. To recall previous commands, you can just press the up arrow key or, in this case, type dir at command prompt as earlier: C:\data\dir. Now you can see that samplefile.txt is present in the directory, as shown in *Figure 5.5.5*:

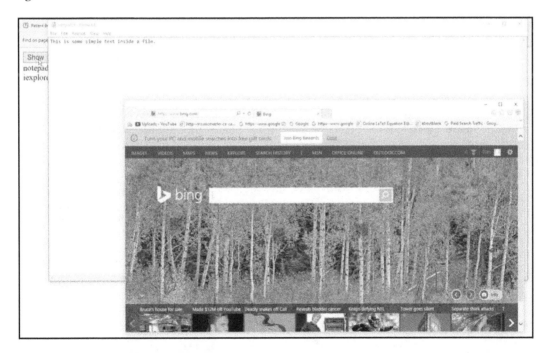

Figure 5.5.5: samplefile.txt is now present in the directory

Now launch this in your browser, and take a look at the results. Click on the **Show** button. It's working as expected: it opened both the Notepad file and the Bing home page, as shown in *Figure 5.5.6*:

Figure 5.5.6: The Notepad file and http://www.bing.com are opened with our program

You can now launch any browser, a process of some kind, directly from your page and show it and you can open up a file, if you want, directly from a browser.

 Note that this works because we are running the page from our local web server and thus we have access to Notepad and the browser. In a real internet application, things would be different.

Also, you can see the listing of the keys, as shown in *Figure 5.5.7*:

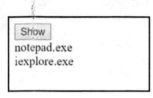

Figure 5.5.7: The listing of the keys

So, these are some of the basics of what you can do with a generic dictionary.

Chapter review

For review, the complete version of the `Default.aspx.cs` file for this chapter, including comments, is shown in the following code block:

```
//using is a directive
//System is a name space
//name space is a collection of features that our needs to run
using System;//needed for EventArgs
using System.Collections.Generic;//needed for dictionary
using System.Diagnostics;//needed for Process.Start
//public means accessible anywhere
//partial means this class is split over multiple files
//class is a keyword and think of it as the outermost level of grouping
//:System.Web.UI.Page means our page inherits the features of a Page
public partial class _Default : System.Web.UI.Page
{
    protected void Button1_Click(object sender, EventArgs e)
    {
        //make a dictionary using string as the type for keys and values
        Dictionary<string, string> filePrograms =
        new Dictionary<string, string>();
        //add two key/value pairs to the dictionary
        filePrograms.Add("notepad.exe", @"c:\data\samplefile.txt");
```

```
fileprograms.Add("iexplore.exe", "http://www.bing.com");
//iterate over the key/value pairs
foreach(KeyValuePair<string, string> kvp in filePrograms)
{
    //invoke Process.Start to launch notepad and internet explorer
    Process.Start(kvp.Key, kvp.Value);
}
//lines below get only at the key inside the filePrograms
//dictionary
foreach(string key in filePrograms.Keys)
{
    sampLabel.Text += $"<br>{key}";
}
    }
}
```

Summary

In this chapter, you learned about generic dictionaries. These are known as key-value pairs. You started a process from a web page, made a verbatim string, iterated over key-value pairs, and made a directory and created a file from command prompt.

In the next chapter, we'll take a look at the connection between delegates and lambda expressions.

6

Connection Between Delegates and Lambda Expressions

In this chapter, we'll take a look at the connection between delegates and Lambda expressions.

Adding a Show Results button to the HTML

Open up a project and, inside the **<html>**, put in a single button that says **Show Results**. To do this, go to **Toolbox** and grab a `Button` control. Drag and drop it below the line beginning with `<form id=`.... You can delete the `<div>` lines as you don't need them. Be sure to insert a `<br>` tag at the end of the line with the button:

```
<asp:Button ID="Button1" runat="server" Text="Show Results" /><br />
```

I'll do a hodgepodge of things just to show you different concepts.

Go to the **Design** view, and double-click on the **Show Results** button. This takes us into `Default.aspx.cs`. Delete the `Page_Load` block. Your initial code screen for this project should look like *Figure 6.1.1*:

```
 1//using is a directive
 2//System is a name space
 3//name space is a collection of features that our needs to run
 4using System;
 5//public means accessible anywhere
 6//partial means this class is split over multiple files
 7//class is a keyword and think of it as the outermost level of grouping
 8//:System.Web.UI.Page means our page inherits the features of a Page
 9public partial class _Default : System.Web.UI.Page
10{
11    protected void Button1_Click(object sender, EventArgs e)
12    {
13
14    }
15}
16
```

Figure 6.1.1: The initial Default.aspx.cs code for this project

Adding delegates

In the first stage, you have to add delegates. While you could put these into a separate file, for our purposes let's just place them here. So, enter the following above the line beginning with `public partial class...`:

```
public delegate bool Compare(double x, double y);
```

Remember, delegates are function or method wrappers, actually. Then, directly below this line, enter the following:

```
public delegate double Multiply(double x, double y);
```

You can see here that we have two delegates. One returns a `Boolean` data type, and the other one returns a `double` data type.

Setting up the variables

Next, inside the event handler for `Button1_Click`, we'll make two variables: x (which we set to 10), and y, which equals 25. So, enter the following between the set of curly braces:

```
double x = 10, y = 25;
```

Making objects of the delegate type

Now, the next thing that we will do is to enter the following below the preceding line:

```
Compare comp = (a, b) => (a == b);
```

As you begin to enter `Compare`, notice from the popup that once you have a delegate (`Compare`), essentially, you can make objects of that kind; then, type `comp`.

Defining lambda expressions

Now, to define a lambda expression, you put = (a,b), as shown. Then this will be mapped to the operations that follow; so you think of => as the mapping symbol or mapping operator. It'll be mapped to the (a==b) operation. So, `comp`, in other words, will allow us to check whether the two values are the same, and that happens in the stage right where a and b are compared. Basically, (a, b) are the parameters, and the expression that is evaluated is whether a is equal to b.

Now, enter the following next:

```
sampLabel.Text = $"{x} and {y} are equal is {comp(x,
y).ToString().ToLower()}";
```

To invoke this, note that you type `comp` and then pass in the x and y values. Then, to show that you can operate on this further, once you get a result from it, you can convert it, say, to a string version, and then all to lowercase, as shown in the preceding code line.

Remember, this is *function chaining*, so it goes from left to right as it executes. In other words, first `comp` runs, then `ToString` and lastly `ToLower`.

Also, note that, at runtime, when you pass in the x and y values when `comp(x, y)` is called, basically, it is (a==b) that will be hit; the comparison will be made, and the value will be sent back.

Next, we can also do the `Multiply` delegate, so enter the following below this line:

```
Multiply mult = (a, b) => (a * b);
```

Notice that `(a,b)` can be used and reused and so on. Remember that `(a,b)` here are parameters, and you can use them and reuse them. They're local within each of the lines where they appear. So, then you can use it in another one. Then, you say again that `(a,b)` maps to an operation of `(a*b)`. Close this with a semicolon.

Now, to invoke this multiplication delegate (Lambda expression that it represents), copy (*Ctrl + C*) the `sampLabel.Text` line from above and paste it (*Ctrl + V*) down below, as shown here:

```
sampLabel.Text += $"<br>{x}*{y} is {mult(x, y).toString()}";
```

Here, we say `{x}*{y}` instead and then, `+=` to append, and delete `are equal`, and replace `comp` with `mult` as the name of our object. You don't need `toString` for it to work, and since it'll give back a number, you don't need `ToLower` either.

Operating an array

Now, in the next stage, another thing that you can do is operate an array. For example, you can make an array of doubles. We'll call it `dubsArray`, and this will be a new `double` array. To do this, enter the following on the next line:

```
double[] dubsArray = new double[] { 1, 2, 3, 4, 5 };
```

Working with actions

Now, we will talk about actions, so enter the following as the next line:

```
Action<double> showDouble = (a) => sampLabel.Text += "<br>" + (a * a);
```

Notice that `Action` is a delegate. So, if you right-click on `Action` and select **Go To Definition**, you'll see `public delegate void Action()`. If you expand it, it says, **Encapsulates a method that has no parameters and does not return a value.** This is the essential definition of an action in .NET.

You can extend an `Action` delegate, however. They can be generic. For example, if you type `Action<double>` and right-click on it and select **Go To Definition** again, this particular form does take a parameter. If you expand it, the **Parameters** section says, **The parameter of the method that this delegate encapsulates**. Further, the *Summary* section says, **Encapsulates a method that has a single parameter and does not return a value**. So, again, there's no need to guess. Right-click and select **Go To Definition** or hover your mouse over it. It tells you what you need to know. In our case, it will actually be `showDouble` as seen in the preceding line. Now, another lambda can be used to define this; so you insert `(a)` there as a single parameter, then, enter the mapping symbol `=>`, and then, `sampLabel.text`. You want to append this to the existing text, so type `+=`, and then, you say, `<br>`, and then show the square of `a`, type `+ (a * a)` and close with a semicolon.

Now remember from the definition of `Actions`, they do not return a value, right? In fact, if we type `Action<double>`, and look at the pop-up tip, if you go through the entire list up through **T16**, it says, **Encapsulates a method that has 16 parameters and does not return a value**, as shown in *Figure 6.1.2*:

```
▲ 16 of 16 ▾ Action<in T1, in T2, in T3, in T4, in T5, in T6, in T7, in T8, in T9, in T10, in T11, in T12, in T13, in T14, in T15, in T16>
            Encapsulates a method that has 16 parameters and does not return a value.
            T2: The type of the second parameter of the method that this delegate encapsulates.
```

Figure 6.1.2. None of the actions return a value after typing Action<double>.

So, none of them return a value. This is a basic feature of `Actions` as they are defined here, but remember that ultimately it's just a delegate.

Then, for example, to make use of these `Actions`, one thing that you can do is to enter the following:

```
foreach(var d in dubsArray)
```

In the next stage, enter the following between a set of curly braces below this line to invoke the actions:

```
showDouble(d);
```

These are the basics of working with delegates and Lambda expressions. The two delegates at the top of the file are the heart of our program, followed by `Compare` and `Multiply`, which are the delegate types being used down below, and then the Lambda expressions, which are parameter expressions, such as `(a, b) => (a == b)`, `(a, b) => (a * b)`, and `(a) => sampLabel.Text += "<br>" + (a * a)`, which are defined using those delegates.

Now, take a look at this in your browser. Click on the **Show Results** button. It says, **10 and 25 are equal is false** and **10*25 is 250**, and then the squares are printed. These are the basic results, and everything looks as it's supposed to look:

Show Results
10 and 25 are equal is false
10*25 is 250
1
4
9
16
25

Figure 6.1.3. The results of running our program

Chapter review

For review purposes, the complete version of the `Default.aspx.cs` file for this chapter, including comments, is shown in the following code block:

```
//using is a directive
//System is a name space
//name space is a collection of features that our needs to run
using System;
//public means accessible anywhere
//partial means this class is split over multiple files
//class is a keyword and think of it as the outermost level of grouping
//:System.Web.UI.Page means our page inherits the features of a Page
public delegate bool Compare(double x, double y);
public delegate double Multiply(double x, double y);
public partial class _Default : System.Web.UI.Page
{
    protected void Button1_Click(object sender, EventArgs e)
    {
        double x = 10, y = 25; //declare two variables
        //the two variables are accessible inside the lambda expressions
        Compare comp = (a, b) => (a == b);//define comparison lambda
        //invoke the lambda in the line below
        sampLabel.Text =
         $"{x} and {y} are equal is {comp(x, y).ToString().ToLower()}";
        //line define a lambda for multiplication
        Multiply mult = (a, b) => (a * b);
        //invoke the multiplication lambda
```

```
sampLabel.Text += $"<br>{x}*{y} is {mult(x, y)}";
//make array of doubles
double[] dubsArray = new double[] { 1, 2, 3, 4, 5 };
//actions encapsulate functions that do not return a value
//but actions can accept arguments to operate on
Action<double> showDouble =
(a) => sampLabel.Text += "&lt;br>" + (a * a);
//it's now possible to perform the action on each d repeatedly
foreach (var d in dubsArray)
{
    showDouble(d);
}
}
}
}
```

Summary

In this chapter, you learned the connection between delegates and lambda expressions. You added delegates, set up the project variables, made objects of the delegate type, operated an array, and worked with `Actions`.

In the next chapter, you will learn about expression-bodied members and then lambda expressions defined by blocks of code.

7
Expression-Bodied Lambdas and Expression-Bodied Members

In this chapter, you will learn about expression-bodied members and then Lambda expressions that are defined by blocks of code.

Adding a box and a Find Max button to the HTML

Bring up a project, and we will set up a box, read three values from this box, and then find the maximum value. We'll also do some other things such as learning how to convert from an array of one data type to another.

Let's begin by typing `Enter Values:` under the line beginning with `<form id=...:`

Then, go to **Toolbox**, grab a `Textbox` control, and put that after **Enter Values:**. You can delete the `<div>` lines as you don't need them. Be sure to insert a `<br>` tag at the end of the line:

```
Enter Values:<asp:TextBox ID="TextBox1" runat="server"></asp:TextBox><br />
```

In the next stage, you'll insert a `Button` control; so get one from the **Toolbox** and drop it below this line. Change the text on the button to say **Find Max**. Again, end the line with a `<br>` tag:

```
<asp:Button ID="Button1" runat="server" Text="Find Max" /><br />
```

Your HTML file for this project should look like *Figure 7.2.1*:

```
 1 <%@ Page Language="C#" AutoEventWireup="true" CodeFile="Default.aspx.cs" Inherits="_Default" %>
 2
 3 <!DOCTYPE html>
 4
 5 <html xmlns="http://www.w3.org/1999/xhtml">
 6 <head runat="server">
 7     <title>Our First Page</title>
 8 </head>
 9 <body>
10     <form id="form1" runat="server">
11     Enter Values:<asp:TextBox ID="TextBox1" runat="server"></asp:TextBox><br />
12         <asp:Button ID="Button1" runat="server" Text="Find Max" /><br />
13         <asp:Label ID="sampLabel" runat="server"></asp:Label>
14
15
16     </form>
17 </body>
18 </html>
19
```

Figure 7.2.1: The HTML file for this project

Now go to the **Design** view. All that we now have is a box and a button, as shown in *Figure 7.2.2*:

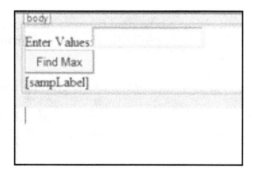

Figure 7.2.2: Our simple interface in the Design view

Next, double-click on the **Find Max** button to go to the `Default.aspx.cs` file, and delete everything. The code in this chapter will be somewhat sophisticated and perhaps a little more challenging than that of previous chapters, but it's the best way to grow and move forward. I will go through the construction of the code line by line. By now, you should be able to see what it takes to begin to program well and how much you have to know.

Making the delegate

Enter `using System` as usual at the very top of the file. Next, to make a delegate, enter the following:

```
delegate double CompareValues(double x, double y);
```

In this line, you have a `delegate` class. It returns a `double` and accepts two `double` data types. So, it encapsulates functions that have that kind of signature.

In the next stage, you'll enter the following within curly braces:

```
public partial class_Default: System.Web.UI.Page
```

This line inherits from `Page` as usual.

Defining an expression-bodied member

In the next stage, we will begin by defining an expression member, so enter the following between a set of curly braces:

```
double FromStringToDouble(string s) => Convert.ToDouble(s);
```

This line shows a new way of creating functions. That's what this is essentially. Instead of putting curly braces within the line, you can now just put something such as a Lambda expression, `=>` in this case. Then the thing to be converted to a `double` data type will be the `s` string. It's also more streamlined; it looks a little more modern, like an expression-bodied member, like a function. Remember that functions are members of classes.

So, in the next stage, we'll define the Button click event below this line. If you go back to the **Design** view and double-click the button, it'll stick in the following line automatically:

```
protected void Button1_Click(object sender, EventArgs e)
```

Next, enter the following between a set of curly braces beneath the preceding line:

```
string[] vals = TextBox1.Text.Split(new char[] { ',' });
```

Converting an array of strings into an array of doubles

Next, let's convert that array of strings into an array of doubles using a different approach; to do this, enter the following below this line:

```
double[] doubleVals = Array.ConvertAll(vals, new Converter<string,
double>(FromStringToDouble));
```

Notice the `ConvertAll` method. It's not so easy to use. You need to have an array on which you'll operate. So, in this case, the array is called `vals`, and then there needs to be something called a *converter object* (note that the popup shows `Converter<TInput, TOutput> converter>`). To make a converter, you enter `new Converter`, and then, in this case, you will transform an array of strings into an array of doubles. So, string is the one you're converting from, and double is the type to which you are converting. This new converter really just wraps a function call, so after that you enter `(FromStringToDouble)`.

The preceding line will accomplish the conversion of the array from one data type to another. Remember, ultimately, it'll grab each value and hit it with `Convert.ToDouble(s)` from the line near the top.

Next, enter the following:

```
CompareValues compareValues = (xin, yin) =>
```

Here, `CompareValues` is a delegate type—it's like a data type—and we'll name it `compareValues`, and then you define a new Lambda `(xin, yin)=>`.

Creating an expression-bodied lambda

Next, you'll define the body of the Lambda. Because this lambda will do several things, you can enclose the body of it within a set of curly braces as follows:

```
{
    double x = xin, y = yin;
}
```

So, this line assigns the values from the parameters above.

Next enter the following directly below this line:

```
return x > y ? x : y;
```

So, if x is greater than y, then return x; otherwise, return y. This is an expression-bodied Lambda, and you close it at the end with a semicolon after the closed curly brace, like this `};`. As you can see, this Lambda expression spans multiple lines. So, you can again inline code just as with the preceding line, using the `double FromStringToDouble(string s) => Convert.ToDouble(s);` function.

Comparing values

In the next stage of the process, we will compare values. To do this, enter the following after the closed curly brace/semicolon beneath the preceding line:

```
sampLabel.Text = CompareValuesInList(compareValues, doubleVals[0],
doubleVals[1], doubleVals[2]).ToString();
```

Here, `CompareValuesInList` is a function that you can create. Then you'll pass in `compareValues`. In other words, when this line says `compareValues`, the entire `CompareValues` block from above will be passed into the body of the function. You've never done this before. You're passing around entire blocks of code! Next, you enter `doubleVals[0]` to get the first value, and then you can copy (*Ctrl + C*) and repeat this for the other ones at index 1 as `doubleVals[1]` and at index 2 as `doubleVals[2]` because there are three of them.

Specifying the parameters

Now, in the next stage, enter the following underneath the closed curly brace after the preceding line:

```
static double CompareValuesInList(CompareValues compFirstTwo, double first,
double second, double third)
```

After `CompareValuesInList`, you'll specify the parameters. So, the first one will be `CompareValues`. This indicates that a delegate can also be used as a type for a parameter. We'll give it the name `compFirstTwo`. Then, you do the `double first`, `double second`, and `double third` parameter. So, there are the three values to be passed in.

Next, enter the following within a set of curly braces beneath the preceding line:

```
return third > compFirstTwo(first, second) ? third : compFirstTwo(first,
second);
```

What this line is saying is that, if `third` is greater than the result of comparing the first two `compFirstTwo(first, second)` parameter—(remember, this expression will run first, and then will return a value comparing the first two—), then it returns the third; otherwise, it will run `compFirstTwo` again and return the bigger of those two.

Running the program

What you have here is very sophisticated code. Now crank it up in your browser, and take a look at the results. Enter some values, say 1,5, and -3, and click on the **Find Max** button. The result is **5**, as you can see in *Figure 7.2.3*:

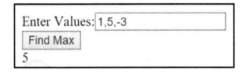

Figure 7.2.3: Preliminary results of running the program with pure integer values

Next, enter something such as 1.01, 1.02, and 0.9999, and click on the **Find Max** button. The result is **1.02**, as you can see in *Figure 7.2.4*:

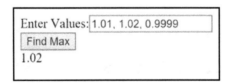

Figure 7.2.4: Results of running the program with extended decimal values

So, the program is working as expected.

Again, to review, because there's a lot of code here, we did the following in this program:

1. First, we declared a delegate.
2. Then we declared an expression-bodied member, which, in this context of this code, is a function that's defined essentially with a Lambda.
3. Next, we made an array of values.

4. Then we created a line to convert the values from a `string` type to a `double` type.

5. After that, we made an expression-bodied Lambda.

6. Then we built a function called `CompareValuesInList` that takes that Lambda as an argument and then also looks at the other values.

7. Finally, `CompareValuesInList` is where the magic really happens, because it says that, if the `third` value is bigger than either of the two first compared, then you return the `third` value. However, if it's not, then simply return the one that is the bigger of the first two.

I know this doesn't seem like an easy thing to do. I know this because I've done this before. You must absolutely add this level of coding, however. Type it, run it, and process it; then you will develop your understanding quickly enough. These are the fundamentals of making some of this stuff useful.

Chapter review

For review, the complete version of the `Default.aspx.cs` file for this chapter, including comments, is shown in the following code block:

```
using System;//needed for array, Convert, and Converter
delegate double CompareValues(double x, double y);//delegate for defining
expression bodied lambda
public partial class _Default :System.Web.UI.Page
{
    double FromStringToDouble(string s) => Convert.ToDouble(s);//expression
bodied function member
    protected void Button1_Click(object sender, EventArgs e)
    {
        //split entries into array of strings
        string[] vals = TextBox1.Text.Split(new char[] { ',' });
        //line 10 below converts all strings to doubles using the
        //vals array, and a new Converter object
        //which really just calls FromStringToDouble
        double[] doubleVals =
        Array.ConvertAll(vals, new Converter<string,
double>(FromStringToDouble));
        //lines 13-17 define the expression bodied lambda, this one
compares two
        //values and returns the bigger
        CompareValues compareValues = (xin, yin) =>
        {
            double x = xin, y = yin;
```

```
        return x > y ? x : y;
    };
    //line 19 invokes CompareValuesInList, which needs the lambda, and
    //list of values to compare
    sampLabel.Text =
    CompareValuesInList(compareValues, doubleVals[0],
doubleVals[1],doubleVals[2]).ToString();
    }
    //lines 22-25 below return either third value if it's biggest,
    //or one of the other two
    static double CompareValuesInList(CompareValues compFirstTwo, double
first, double second, double    third)
    {
        return third > compFirstTwo(first, second) ? third :
compFirstTwo(first, second);
    }
}
```

Summary

In this chapter, you learned about expression-bodied members and then Lambda expressions, which are defined by blocks of code. You made a delegate, defined an expression-bodied member, converted an array of strings into an array of doubles, created an expression-bodied lambda, and built the code to compare values and specified parameters.

In the next chapter, you will learn about anonymous functions.

8

Anonymous Methods and Objects That Run Their Own Delegates

In this chapter, we will talk about anonymous functions.

Adding a Show Results button to the HTML

Open up a project and, inside the **<html>**, put in a single button that says Show Results. For this, go to the **Toolbox** and grab a Button control. Drag and drop it below the line beginning with <form id=.... You can delete the <div> lines, as you don't need them. Be sure to insert a <br> tag at the end of the Button line.

```
<asp:Button ID="Button1" runat="server" Text="Show Results" /><br />
```

Next, we will display some results to the user. To do this, go to the **Design** view, and double-click on the **Show Results** button. This takes us into `Default.aspx.cs`. Delete the `Page_Load` block. The relevant portion of the starting code for this project should look like *Figure 8.3.1*:

```
 1 //using is a directive
 2 //System is a name space
 3 //name space is a collection of features that our needs to run
 4 using System;
 5 //public means accessible anywhere
 6 //partial means this class is split over multiple files
 7 //class is a keyword and think of it as the outermost level of grouping
 8 //:System.Web.UI.Page means our page inherits the features of a Page
 9 public partial class _Default : System.Web.UI.Page
10 {
11
12 protected void Button1_Click(object sender, EventArgs e)
13     {
14
15     }
16 }
17
```

Figure 8.3.1: The starting code section for this project

Streamlining writing functions

Within the body, but above the line beginning with `protected void Button1_Click...`, enter the following:

```
private void ShowSquare(double x) => sampLabel.Text += "<br>" + (x * x);
```

Remember, `=>` is an *expression member*. It's a function. In other words, it takes the form of a Lambda. At the end of the line, we return x * x. As you can see, this is a very streamlined way of writing functions.

Next, we need to add namespaces. So, after `using System`, enter the following lines:

```
using System.Collections.Generic;
using System.Threading;
```

Now, within the event for the button, we will place the following code list; so, enter this line between a set of curly braces underneath the line beginning with `protected void Button1_Click...`:

```
List<double> vals = new List<double>(new double[] { 1, 2, 4, 5, 6, 8 });
```

In this line, you are making a new list of `double` data type and then you will initialize it. You can do this a couple of ways, but you can just write an array and then enter some values. It doesn't really matter what they are. This will make a list of `double` data types.

Performing an action on all of the values

Now, one thing that you can do is to perform an action on all the values. So, the way to do that is to enter the following:

```
vals.ForEach(ShowSquare);
```

This is how you can call `ShowSquare` on each value. Notice that, in this case, `ShowSquare` is named. `ShowSquare` represents this expression, `sampLabel.Text += "<br>" + (x * x);` so it's a *named quantity*.

Making an anonymous function or method

Now, if you want, you can also do stuff that does not involve names. For example, you can enter the following next:

```
vals.ForEach(delegate (double x)
```

Next, we'll define the body, or the logic, between a set of curly braces. This is a nameless or *anonymous* one. For example, you can enter the following below this line (notice that you close with a parenthesis and semicolon after the closed curly brace):

```
{
    sampLabel.Text += "<br>" + Math.Pow(x, 3);
});
```

This one does something similar to the previous line. The only difference is that we are not calling anything named; we are just defining an *anonymous function*, a nameless function using a `delegate` keyword. This does accept one value, of course, the x value. Then you cube the x value; `Math.Pow(x, 3)` means, cube it and then display it on the label using `+=` to append and `<br>` to push down a line, as usual.

Now, in the next stage, you can also do stuff such as the following, which is quite interesting:

```
Thread td = new Thread(delegate ())
```

Believe it or not, though it isn't recommended, after `new Thread` you can even can type `dele` instead of `delegate`, in this case.

Now, when you make an object of this type, you can also create a delegate. So, when you make this `Thread` object, you're also making an anonymous function. In other words, you're sending a piece of processing so that it runs on its own thread, and then you can stick in stuff such as the following:

```
{
List<double> arrs = new List<double>(new double[] { 1, 4, 5, 3, 53, 52
});arrs.Sort();arrs.ForEach(x => sampLabel.Text += $"<br>{x}");
});
```

Note again that here you close with a parenthesis and semicolon after the closing curly brace.

Starting a thread

Now, with threads like this, you get a thread started on the next line as follows:

```
td.Start();
```

This will start the thread in its own little separate piece of processing, separate from the main program so to speak.

So, the big idea here is that this anonymous stuff is quite powerful. For example, you can build an anonymous function or method such as the preceding one we created. It runs, but it's not named, and basically, even when you make a new `Thread` object, you can make a delegate. In other words, it can do a bit of processing of its own and you don't have to put this off into other functions or anything like that.

Running and modifying the program

Now, let's run the program. For this, crank it up in your browser and click on the **Show Results** button. Take a look at the results, as shown in *Figure 8.3.2*. There's one slight issue with the program as it's written. We will learn the reason for this problem momentarily and then fix it:

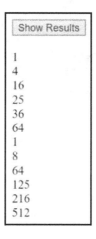

Figure 8.3.2: The initial run of our program

Now, there's one more function I want to tell you about, `Join`. Enter the following as the next line:

```
td.Join();
```

Now, if you hover your mouse over `Join`, the pop-up tip says **Blocks the calling thread until the thread terminates, while continuing to perform standard COM and Send, Message Pumping**. If you hover your mouse over `Start`, the pop-up tip says **Causes the operating system to change the state of the current instance to ThreadState.Running**. In other words, in the `Thread td = new Thread(delegate ()` block, `Thread` is an object. In this case, you're making a new thread that has a delegate, so it runs off in its own thread of processing, away from the main program. So, it's kind of interesting.

Now, notice that, when we printed that stuff, there were only really two main lists, with the second one essentially appended to the first. So, let's do it this way; otherwise, we will not be able to see the effect clearly. Under the preceding `vals.ForEach(ShowSquare)` line, enter the following:

```
sampLabel.Text += "<br>---------------------------------------------------
--";
```

Note that I separated this with a long-dashed line in quotes.

Next, after this one, let's do one more beneath the closing curly brace, parenthesis, and semicolon after the `sampLabel.Text += "<br>"` + `Math.Pow(x, 3)` line.

```
sampLabel.Text += "<br>---------------------------------------------------
---";
```

Now, if we remove `td.Join()` and run the program, there are only two lists, as shown in *Figure 8.3.3*. There should be three of them, however:

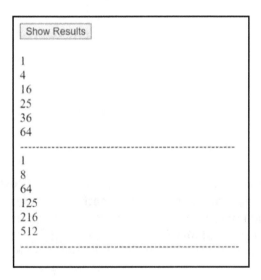

Figure 8.3.3: The modified run shows only two lists

So re-insert `td.Join();` and take a look at it again in your browser. Now, as you can see in *Figure 8.3.4*, there are three lists, as there should be:

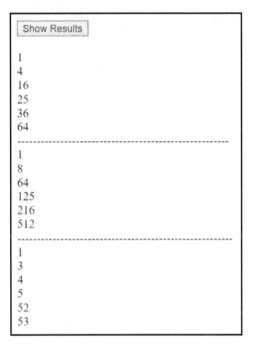

Figure 8.3.4: The final program run shows three separate lists

Again to review, we did the following in this program:

1. First, we called the `vals.ForEach(ShowSquare)` bit, which generates a list.
2. Then we called the block beginning with `vals.ForEach(delegate (double x)`, as an anonymous function or method that generates a list.
3. Next, with the block beginning with `Thread td = new Thread(delegate (),` we created this anonymous object called `td`, which is a `Thread` class that has its own anonymous method inside, which runs in its own separate thread.
4. Finally, we started it, and the `Join` function blocks the current thread, waiting for the `Thread td = new Thread(delegate ()` block to execute, and then it resumed, so that everything was displayed.

These are the fundamentals of anonymous constructs of this kind.

Chapter review

For review, the complete version of the `Default.aspx.cs` file for this chapter, including comments, is shown in the following code block:

```
//using is a directive
//System is a name space
//name space is a collection of features that our needs to run
using System;
using System.Collections.Generic;
using System.Threading;
//public means accessible anywhere
//partial means this class is split over multiple files
//class is a keyword and think of it as the outermost level of grouping
//:System.Web.UI.Page means our page inherits the features of a Page
public partial class _Default : System.Web.UI.Page
{
    private void ShowSquare(double x) =>
    sampLabel.Text += "<br>" + (x * x);//expression bodied function
    protected void Button1_Click(object sender, EventArgs e)
    {
        //make list of double values
        List<double> vals =
        new List<double>(new double[] { 1, 2, 4, 5, 6, 8 });
        //call ShowSquare on each value inside the list
        vals.ForEach(ShowSquare);
        sampLabel.Text += "<br>--------------------------------------" ;
        //lines 21-24 define an unnamed method, which is applied to each
        //value in the list
        vals.ForEach(delegate (double x)
        {
            sampLabel.Text += "<br>" + Math.Pow(x, 3);
        });
        sampLabel.Text += "<br>--------------------------------------" ;
        //lines 28-35 create a thread object, and an unnamed method inside
        //it that spawns
        //a thread of processing separate from the "main" program
        Thread td = new Thread(delegate ()
        {
            List<double> arrs =
            new List<double>(new double[] { 1, 4, 5, 3, 53, 52 });
            arrs.Sort();
            arrs.ForEach(x => sampLabel.Text += $"<br>{x}");
        });
        //start the thread
        td.Start();
        td.Join(); //this is needed to ensure that the thread
```

```
            //"td" runs, and then joins back to the
            //current, main thread, so the program finishes running
        }
    }
```

Summary

In this chapter, you learned about anonymous functions. You streamlined writing functions, performed an action on all of the values, made an anonymous function or method, and started a thread.

In the next chapter, we will take a look at the basics of languages: Language Integrated Query. It's a powerful way of manipulating data directly within your C# code.

9
C# with LINQ and Built-In Types

In this chapter, we will talk about the basics of LINQ. You will learn how to use LINQ or Language Integrated Query. It's a powerful way of manipulating data directly within your C# code.

Adding a Show Values button to the HTML

Bring up a project, and below the line beginning with `<form id=...` in the **<html>**, we will place a button. Change the text on the button to something different, for example, **Show Values**.

Now switch to the **Design** view, and double-click on the **Show Values** button. This takes us into `Default.aspx.cs`. Delete the `Page_Load` block. We don't need it. The relevant portion of the starting code for this project should look like *Figure 9.4.1*:

```
1 //using is a directive
2 //System is a name space
3 //name space is a collection of features that our needs to run
4 using System;
5 //public means accessible anywhere
6 //partial means this class is split over multiple files
7 //class is a keyword and think of it as the outermost level of grouping
8 //:System.Web.UI.Page means our page inherits the features of a Page
9 public partial class _Default : System.Web.UI.Page
10 {
11     protected void Button1_Click(object sender, EventArgs e)
12     {
13
14     }
15 }
16
```

Figure 9.4.1: The starting code section for this project

We'll work with a little bit of code in this chapter, but it's sequential from top to bottom.

Adding namespaces

The first thing to do is to add two new namespaces; so, enter the following after `using System`:

```
using System.Linq;
using System.Collections.Generic;
```

LINQ stands for Language Integrated Query, and `using System.Collections .Generic` is for working with lists. These are the two new namespaces that we are using.

Working with the IEnumerable generic interface

Next, in between the set of curly braces beneath the line beginning with `protected void Button1_Click...`, the first thing that we will do is create an array of names. For this, enter the following:

```
IEnumerable<string> names = new string[] { "john", "job", "janet", "mary",
"steve" };
```

Let's name it `names`, and then say, create a `new string` array. Then, to specify the initializer list, we enter a series of names in quotes, and close this with a semicolon.

Now notice that, on the left-hand side, we have `IEnumerable`. This is a generic interface. As you can see, the `new string` array in this line can be created this way because it's possible to take an array then step through it, so that each entry inside the array is a string. So, it's `IEnumerable`: we can list values within it, and each value to be listed is a string. To enumerate means to list.

Converting an array to a list of integers

Next, enter the following below this line:

```
List<int> lst = new int[] { 1, 2, 12, 4, 5, -10, 5, 25, 54 }.ToList();
```

To make a list of integers, we say `lst = new int[]`. Then we specify the initializer list and the values shown here. It doesn't matter what values you use. I'll show you some of the methods. Of course, as you can imagine, there are many of them.

Now, note that you could not stop writing this line after the array. If you did, the pop-up tip would say **Cannot implicitly convert type 'int[]' System.Collections.Generic.List<int>'**; so you have to add `.ToList()`. You can convert an array to a list of integers.

Determining the values in a collection

Now that we have collections of items to go through, we can do that. To do this, enter the following:

```
IEnumerable<int> valuesMoreThanTen = lst.Where(x => x >10);
```

Here, we first operate on the list of numerical values, so we say `valuesMoreThanTen`. To make this happen, you enter the name of the list, which is `lst`. Notice in the pop-up tip all of the functions that have become available. One of them is `Where<>`. After you select `Where<>`, you can specify a condition that applies, in our case, where `x` is such that `x` is greater than `10`, or `(x => x > 10)`, and close this with a semicolon.

If you hover your mouse over `Where`, and look where it says `IEnumerable<int>`, it says that it returns, in other words, an `IEnumerable` construct, which we can iterate through with a `foreach` loop, for example. Further, it says `(Func<int,bool>`... and then there is a `predicate` delegate. So, we will take each value and we'll basically apply some action to it. We'll check whether some condition holds: either the condition holds on it or it doesn't.

As you can see, we basically have LINQ, and then we have inside that, a Lambda expression. So, to make use of it, you'll enter the following next:

```
valuesMoreThanTen.ToList().ForEach(x => sampLabel.Text += $"<br>x={x}");
```

Converting the values back to a list

After `valuesMoreThanTen`, you would like to be able to use a `foreach` loop. To do this, you've got to convert this back to a list because, remember, `IEnumerable` is not a list. That's why the `foreach` loop doesn't show if you typed it right after the . (dot) after `valuesMoreThanTen`. You convert it to a list, and then `foreach` shows. Now you can again display the values; so in `foreach x`, you'll take the `x` value and display it in a label as shown in the preceding line of code. This line now will display each `x` value from the `valuesMoreThanTen` list.

Now, you can tell just by examining it that `12`, `25`, and `54` should print. That's the first thing. Now, let's also display a horizontal line below this line. So, enter the following next:

```
sampLabel.Text += "<br><hr/>";
```

Extracting values from the list and sorting them

Now, imagine that you have this array of names, and you want to extract those that, for example, have a j letter, and then sort them from, say, the shortest to the longest. These are the kinds of things that you can do when you operate on data. So, enter the following next:

```
IEnumerable<string> namesWithJSorted = names.Where(name =>
name.Contains("j")).OrderBy(name => name.Length);
```

Again, IEnumerable is of the string type in this line. That's why we mean that IEnumerable is generic, because it operates on integers, and string and so on. Next, you say namesWithJSorted, and I've named this variable this particular way because the functions will be chained from left to right. So, you type the name of the names array, and then you type Where(name => name.Contains("j") in order to check each name to see if it contains the letter j. Then further, once you have all of those names that contain a letter j, you'll order that result by the length of each name with OrderBy(name => name.Length).

Again, from left to right you can chain these functions. This is LINQ. As you can see inside each one, you basically have a Lambda expression: Where and then, OrderBy. It's powerful, right?

Next, to display it, remember, because namesWithJSorted is IEnumerable, you can convert it back to a list and then use foreach; or, if you want, you can just type the following:

```
foreach(var str in namesWithJSorted)
{
    sampLabel.Text += $"<br>{str}";
}
```

Remember, in the directly preceding line, += is to append, $ is for string interpolation, and <br> is there to push down a line. The actual value to be printed appears within the curly braces.

These are the basics of these concepts.

Running the program

Now, we have to confirm that this will work as expected. So, crank it up in your browser, and click on the **Show Values** button. As you can see in *Figure 9.4.2*, it displays **x=12**, **x=25**, and **x=54**, and then below that it displays the names **job**, **john**, and **janet**. Each name contains a j letter, and they are listed from shortest to longest, as expected:

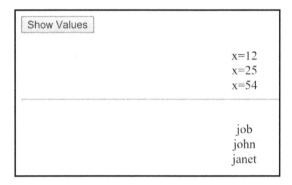

Figure 9.4.2: The results of running the program for this chapter

Remember, this is basically a combination. You have a Lambda expression, (x => x > 10), and then you stick that into a method such as `where` or `OrderBy`. When you combine the two, the code becomes very powerful, as you can see, and very expressive, letting you accomplish a lot. Also, remember that on the left-hand side, many of the results in LINQ return items of the `IEnumerable` type.

Chapter review

For review, the complete version of the `Default.aspx.cs` file for this chapter, including comments, is shown in the following code block:

```
//using is a directive
//System is a name space
//name space is a collection of features that our needs to run
using System;
using System.Linq;
using System.Collections.Generic;
//public means accessible anywhere
//partial means this class is split over multiple files
//class is a keyword and think of it as the outermost level of grouping
//:System.Web.UI.Page means our page inherits the features of a Page
public partial class _Default : System.Web.UI.Page
```

```
{
    protected void Button1_Click(object sender, EventArgs e)
    {
        //line 16 creates array of names
        IEnumerable<string> names = new string[] { "john", "job", "janet",
        "mary", "steve" };
        //line 18 creates array of integers, and converts to
        //list of integers
        List<int> lst = new int[] { 1, 2, 12, 4, 5, -10, 5, 25, 54
}.ToList();
        //line below puts a lambda expression inside Where to
        //create a query
        IEnumerable<int> valuesMoreThanTen = lst.Where(x => x > 10);
        //line 22 prints the results from lines 20 above
        valuesMoreThanTen.ToList().ForEach(x => sampLabel.Text +=
$"<br>x={x}");
        sampLabel.Text += "<br><hr/>";
        //line 25 below chains functions, going from left to right, to
        //produce a list of names with j, sorted by length
        IEnumerable<string> namesWithJSorted =
        names.Where(name => name.Contains( "j")).OrderBy
        (name => name.Length);
        //lines below display the names that are generated line 25 above
        foreach (var str in namesWithJSorted)
        {
            sampLabel.Text += $"<br>{str}";
        }
    }
}
```

Summary

In this chapter, we talked about the basics of LINQ. You learned how to use LINQ, or Language Integrated Query. It's a powerful way of manipulating data directly within your C# code. You added namespaces, worked with the IEnumerable generic interface, converted an array into a list of integers, determined the values within a collection, converted those values back to a list, and extracted those values from the list and sorted them.

In the next chapter, we will talk about using LINQ with custom types.

10
C# with LINQ and Custom Data Types

In this chapter, we will talk about using LINQ with custom types.

Adding a Show People button to the HTML

Bring up a project. Go to `Default.aspx`, and below the line that begins with with `<form id=...`, put in a button. To do this, go to the **Toolbox**, grab a `Button` control, and drag it in there. Change the text on the button to say **Show People**:

```
<asp:Button ID="Button1" runat="server" Text="Show People" />
```

Setting up a database

We will have a database, we will query it, and we will show people who have, for example, a certain letter in their names, make a certain amount of money, and sort it in a certain way.

To accomplish this, go to the **Design** view, and double-click on the **Show People** button. This takes us into `Default.aspx.cs`. Delete the `Page_Load` block. The relevant portion of the starting code for this project should look like *Figure 10.5.1*:

```
1 //using is a directive
2 //System is a name space
3 //name space is a collection of features that our needs to run
4 using System;
5 //public means accessible anywhere
6 //partial means this class is split over multiple files
7 //class is a keyword and think of it as the outermost level of grouping
8 //:System.Web.UI.Page means our page inherits the features of a Page
9 public partial class _Default : System.Web.UI.Page
10 {
11     protected void Button1_Click(object sender, EventArgs e)
12     {
13
14     }
15 }
16
```

Figure 10.5.1: The starting code section for this project

In the next stage, first go to the top of the file, and enter the following after `using System`:

```
using System.Linq;
```

Next, we'll make a class. We'll call it `Person`. So, above the line beginning with `public partial class...`, insert the following:

```
public class Person
```

Making a custom type using LINQ

Now, between the set of curly braces below the preceding line, you will declare two auto properties, as follows:

```
public string Name { get; set; }
public decimal Salary { get; set; }
```

Then, to make a constructor, enter the following below these lines:

```
public Person(string name, decimal salary)
```

Next, you will set the values of the properties inside the constructor. So, enter the following between a set of curly braces below these lines:

```
Name = name; Salary = salary;
```

This is our simple custom type, `Person`, with two automatic properties in a parameterized constructor.

Setting up an array of people

In the next stage, you'll make an array of people; enter the following between a set of curly braces below the line beginning with `protected void Button1_Click....`:

```
Person[] people = new Person[] { new Person("John", 76877), new
Person("Bobby", 78988), new Person("Joan", 87656) };
```

Querying the array

Now, to query this, enter the following below this line:

```
IEnumerable<Person> peopleWithN = people.Where(per =>
per.Name.EndsWith("n")).OrderByDescending(per => per.Salary);
```

As you type, notice that `IEnumerable` doesn't show up, so you've got to go to the top of the file again and enter the following after `using System.Linq`:

```
using System.Collections.Generic;
```

Now let's make use of this down below; so, underneath the line beginning with `Person[]` `people...`, enter the line `IEnumerable<Person>...` stated earlier.

Here, `Person` is a type of object that can be enumerated from the list of people. `peopleWithN` indicates that we'll be searching for people who have an n letter in their name. In fact, the code searches for people whose name ends with n. (Note that `per` stands for each person inside the list.) Further, we sort by salaries in descending order.

Because people sometimes type information inconsistently, you first have to convert everything to the equivalent case, but this is something for you to figure out on your own.

Remember, in this line we have `people`, which is the name of some kind of object, and `Where`, an extension method, followed by a Lambda. Next, we use `OrderByDescending`, which you can select that from the list of methods, to order values, such as a person's salary, in descending order.

So, the purpose of this line is to choose each person whose name ends with `n`, and then order the results by salary. This yields an `IEnumerable` object, and now you can step through it, of course, and say the following in the next line:

```
foreach(Person p in peopleWithN)
```

Now, to print it all, enter the following between a set of curly braces below this line:

```
sampLabel.Text += $"<br>{p.Name} {p.Salary:C}";
```

Here, we put the `Name` variable first, and the `Salary` variable formatted as Currency.

Running the program

This is the heart of our program. Crank it up in your browser. Click on the **Show People** button, and the results are displayed, as shown in *Figure 10.5.2*:

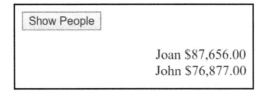

Figure 10.5.2: The results of running the program

So, Joan makes $87,656.00 and John makes $76,877.00. They were selected because both of them have names ending in a lowercase **n**, as you can see, and then it's sorted by salary in descending order. So, it's working as expected. As you can see, you can also define custom types, such as the one within curly braces below `public class Person`, using LINQ. It is very powerful and works well.

Chapter review

For review, the complete version of the `Default.aspx.cs` file for this chapter, including comments, is shown in the following code block:

```
//using is a directive
//System is a name space
//name space is a collection of features that our needs to run
using System;
using System.Linq;
using System.Collections.Generic;
//public means accessible anywhere
//partial means this class is split over multiple files
//class is a keyword and think of it as the outermost level of grouping
//:System.Web.UI.Page means our page inherits the features of a Page
public class Person
{
    public string Name { get; set; } //auto implemented properties
    public decimal Salary { get; set; }
    public Person(string name, decimal salary)
    {
        Name = name; Salary = salary;//set values of properties
    }
}
public partial class _Default : System.Web.UI.Page
{
    protected void Button1_Click(object sender, EventArgs e)
    {
        //make array of people
        Person[] people = new Person[] { new Person("John", 76877),
                                new Person("Bobby",78988),
                                new Person("Joan", 87656) };
        //find all people with "n" as the last letter, and then display
        //the results sorted from high to low salary
        IEnumerable<Person> peopleWithN =
        people.Where(per => per.Name.EndsWith("n")).OrderByDescending
        (per => per.Salary);
        //display name and salary formatted as currency
        foreach (Person p in peopleWithN)
        {
            sampLabel.Text += $"<br>{p.Name} {p.Salary:C}";
        }
    }
}
```

Summary

In this chapter, we talked about using LINQ with custom types. You set up a database, made a custom type using LINQ, set up an array of people, and queried the array.

In the next chapter, you will learn how to write queries using query syntax.

11

Using Query Syntax to Construct Queries

In this chapter, you will learn how to write queries using query syntax, for example, method chaining, as we done have before.

Adding a show button to the HTML

Bring up a project and the only thing that will go into the **<html>** is a button and nothing else. To do this, go to **Toolbox**, grab a `Button` control, and drag and drop it below the line beginning with `<form id=`.... Replace the text on the button to say **Show**:

```
<asp:Button ID="Button1" runat="server" Text="Show" />
```

Now, switch to the **Design** view, and double-click on the **Show** button. This takes us into `Default.aspx.cs`. Delete the event handling stub. The relevant portion of the starting code for this project should look like *Figure 11.6.1*:

```
 1 //using is a directive
 2 //System is a name space
 3 //name space is a collection of features that our needs to run
 4 using System;
 5 //public means accessible anywhere
 6 //partial means this class is split over multiple files
 7 //class is a keyword and think of it as the outermost level of grouping
 8 //:System.Web.UI.Page means our page inherits the features of a Page
 9 public partial class _Default : System.Web.UI.Page
10 {
11     protected void Button1_Click(object sender, EventArgs e)
12     {
13
14     }
15 }
16
```

Figure 11.6.1: The starting code section for this project

Next, go to the top of the file and, under `using System`, enter the following:

```
using System.Collections.Generic;
using System.Linq;
```

To make use of this, we'll do what follows. It's routine code; it's mechanical. The first thing is that, when somebody clicks on the **Show** button, you want to create a label so that there's a cumulative output all the time. To do this, enter the following between the curly braces under the line beginning with `protected void Button1_Click...`:

```
sampLabel.Text = "";
```

Creating a decimal salary array

Next, below the preceding line, you'll make a `decimal` array called `salaries`, naturally enough. So, enter the following:

```
decimal[] salaries = new decimal[] { 56789, 78888, 35555, 34533, 75000 };
```

This is how you can query a `decimal` array. This is a `decimal` array specifically, but it could be any array essentially. We throw in some values, and there you go.

Working with range variables

Next, enter the following below this line:

```
IEnumerable<string> salResults = from salary in salaries
```

Notice that the return or results set will be of the `string` type, not of the `decimal` type. After `salResults =`, you want to define the body of the LINQ queries, so you say `from salary in salaries`. If you hover your mouse over `salary` here, you see that it is what is known as a *range variable*, shown in *figure 11.6.2*. So, you're asking it to take a look in `salaries`. As a range variable, it's the quantity that goes over all of the entries individually.

```
IEnumerable<string> salResults = from salary in salaries
                    where 356                              00
                    orderby s    ●  (range variable) decimal salary
                    select $"<br>{salary:C}";
```

Figure 11.6.2: Range variable

Selecting a salary range and putting it in descending order

Now you'll specify some kind of logical condition. For example, to filter the results in some fashion. So, enter the following, indented, under this line:

```
where 35000 <= salary && salary <= 75000
select $"<br>{salary:C}";
```

Next, you can `orderby` the result set to list salaries in descending order, for example; so, enter the following directly under this line:

```
orderby salary descending
```

The default is in ascending order, from small to big, and you want to reverse that. When you throw in the `descending` keyword, then it goes from big to small.

Next, remember the objective is to get an `IEnumerable` construct of strings filled with strings. So, finally, enter the following as part of this block:

```
select $"<br>{salary:C}";
```

You can also format the results in place, as I've done in this line, for example, in currency format.

Displaying the results

With this block of code in place, the next stage, of course, is to iterate over this and display the results. For this, you can go with a conversion to a list and print, or you can just do the following next:

```
foreach(string formattedSalary in salResults)
```

How do we know that we should say string in this line? Remember that the preceding IEnumerable line is filled with strings, correct? If you hover your mouse over IEnumerable, it says IEnumerable<out T>, and T is string.

Now, to display the results, enter the following between a set of curly braces beneath the preceding line:

```
sampLabel.Text += formattedSalary;
```

Here, formattedSalary is what is to be displayed.

Now, crank this up in your browser. Click on the **Show** button. The results appear, as shown in *Figure 11.6.3*:

Figure 11.6.3: The initial results of running the program

The salaries here are sorted in descending order, from highest to lowest, and they fall within the $75,000 to $35,000 range. So, that's working as expected.

Observing deferred execution

Now, one thing that you should be aware of is the concept called *deferred execution*. So, to see what that means, take a look at what follows.

Imagine that I place a break point right at the `foreach(string formattedSalary in salResults)` line. Then, select **Step Into** from the **Debug** menu and click on the **Show** button. Note how each line runs consecutively (the elapsed time in ms appears after each line). You should see how it's going into it; how it's running.

One thing that you should be aware of with LINQ is the concept of deferred execution, which means that, `salResults` actually runs, as you can see, so it's a query variable essentially. It runs when you iterate over it using a `foreach` construct, as shown in the following code block, not when you write it in the preceding `IEnumerable` block. It doesn't run then. It runs when you iterate over it. Otherwise, your program will potentially carry huge amounts of information in these query results. So, that's about deferred execution:

```
IEnumerable<string> salResults = from salary in salaries
                                 where 35000 <= salary && salary <= 75000
                                 orderby salary descending
                                 select $"<br>{salary:C}";
foreach(string formattedSalary in salResults)
{
    //display formatted salaries one at a time
    sampLabel.Text += formattedSalary;
}
```

In the next stage, we'll take a look at another practical example of what you might be able to do. We also want to display horizontal lines, so enter the following after the closed curly brace below the `sampLabel.Text += formattedSalary` line:

```
sampLabel.Text += "<br><hr/>";
```

The `<hr/>` tag will add a horizontal line to the output.

Making a dictionary

Next, we'll make a `Dictionary`; for this, enter the following line next:

```
Dictionary<string, decimal> nameSalaries = new Dictionary<string,
decimal>();
```

Here, `<string,decimal>` represents the key-value pairs.

Working with key-value pairs

Now, let's add some key-value pairs. So, start by entering the following:

```
nameSalaries.Add("John Jones", 45355);
```

In this line, `John Jones` is the key and the value is his salary or $45,355.

Then, you can repeat this a couple of times, so copy and paste this line three more times directly underneath it. Say, John Smith, 76900; John Jenkins, 89000; and Steve Jobs, 98000:

```
nameSalaries.Add("John Smith", 76900);
nameSalaries.Add("John Jenkins", 89000);
nameSalaries.Add("Steve Jobs", 98000);
```

Note that I repeated the name *John* here a couple of times, because I wanted to illustrate a concept shortly. The last one listed is *Steve Jobs* and of course his salary was much more than 98000!

Querying the data in the key-value pairs

Now, again we will query this. This is the data that we have in key-value pairs and we'll query it. So, enter the following below these lines:

```
var dictResults = from nameSalary in nameSalaries
```

Here, `nameSalary` is a range variable, which refers to John Jones, John Smith, John Jenkins, Steve Jobs, and so on, and `nameSalaries` is the dictionary itself. `nameSalary` is the particular combination of a key and a value.

Next, underneath this line, indent the following code:

```
where nameSalary.Key.Contains("John") && nameSalary.Value >= 65000
```

Here we're saying where the key contains the name John, and the salary is greater than or equal to $65,000. If you wanted to, you could add `OrderBy` and so on, but for our purposes, enter the following directly below this line:

```
select $"<br>{nameSalary.Key} earns {nameSalary.Value:C} per year.";
```

In this line, we will select those records that apply in the case of these two conditions: the name is John and the salary exceeds $65,000. So, in our case, that would definitely be John Smith and John Jenkins. To format the output so that it looks good, we say `nameSalary.Value:C` to format it as currency and then add `per year`.

Now, hover your mouse over `dictResults`. Do you see where it says `IEnumerable` in the tooltip popup? Now, `var` is called *implicit typing*. We've seen `var` before. Sometimes it's difficult to tell what the output will be from a query like the one we created, which is sufficiently complicated. So, if you do implicit typing, it tells you what the output should be, so `IEnumerable` of the `string` type. Now if you wanted to, you can change this line as follows:

```
IEnumerable<string> dictResults = from nameSalary in nameSalaries
```

Now we also know this because at the end of this query, you see that there are strings, correct? These are strings that include formatting information and now, of course, you can iterate over this as usual; so, enter the following next:

```
foreach(string nameSal in dictResults)
```

Then, between a set of curly braces under this line, finish with the following:

```
sampLabel.Text += nameSal;
```

Running the program

Run this in your browser to make sure that it's working as expected. Click on the **Show** button. The results are shown in *Figure 11.6.4*:

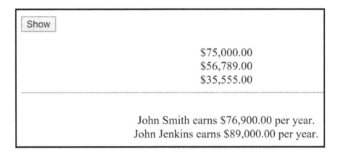

Figure 11.6.4: The results of running our program

Now you've got the first results that I described earlier and the second set of results are displayed below them, showing that both names contain John and the amounts are $65,000 or more.

Chapter review

For review, the complete version of the `Default.aspx.cs` file for this chapter, including comments, is shown in the following code block:

```
//using is a directive
//System is a name space
//name space is a collection of features that our needs to run
using System;
using System.Collections.Generic;
using System.Linq;
//public means accessible anywhere
//partial means this class is split over multiple files
//class is a keyword and think of it as the outermost level of grouping
//:System.Web.UI.Page means our page inherits the features of a Page
public partial class _Default : System.Web.UI.Page
{
    protected void Button1_Click(object sender, EventArgs e)
    {
        //clear label on button click
        sampLabel.Text = "";
        //make array of salaries
        decimal[] salaries =
```

```
new decimal[] { 56789, 78888, 35555, 34533, 75000 };
//construct Linq query, which produces a collection of
//formatted strings
IEnumerable<string> salResults = from salary in salaries
                    where 35000 <= salary && salary <= 75000
                    orderby salary descending
                    select $"<br>{salary:C}";
foreach(string formattedSalary in salResults)
{
    //display formatted salaries one at a time
    sampLabel.Text += formattedSalary;
}
//show horizontal rule on screen
sampLabel.Text += "<br><hr/>";
//make dictionary to hold names and salaries as key/value pairs
Dictionary<string, decimal> nameSalaries =
new Dictionary<string, decimal>();
nameSalaries.Add("John Jones", 45355);
nameSalaries.Add("John Smith", 76900);
nameSalaries.Add("John Jenkins", 89000);
nameSalaries.Add("Steve Jobs", 98000);
//query below represents all people named John who make 65000
//and more
//this query gives back a formatted string for each key/value
//pair that
//satisfies the condition
IEnumerable<string> dictResults = from nameSalary in nameSalaries
                    where nameSalary.Key.Contains("John") &&
                    nameSalary.Value >= 65000
                    select $"<br>{nameSalary.Key} earns
                    {nameSalary.Value:C} per year.";
foreach(string nameSal in dictResults)
{
    sampLabel.Text += nameSal;//display named and salaries
}
    }
}
```

Summary

In this chapter, you learned how to write queries using query syntax. You created a decimal salary array, worked with range variables, observed deferred execution, made a dictionary, worked with key-value pairs, queried the data in the key-value pairs, and learned about implicit typing.

In the next chapter, we will explore LINQ further. Specifically, we'll take a look at some of the power of LINQ to perform aggregation functions, such as averaging, summation, and counting. Also, we'll talk about lists of lists, which are very practical thing.

12
Queries That Perform Aggregation Functions

In this chapter, we will explore LINQ further. Specifically, we'll look at the power of LINQ to perform, for example, aggregation functions like averaging, summation, counting, and so on. Also, we'll talk about lists of lists, which is a very practical thing.

Adding a show button to the HTML

Bring up project and, to keep things brief, all we will do is put in a button below the line beginning with `<form id=`..... To do this, go to **Toolbox**, grab a `Button` control, and drag it in there. Change the text on the Button to say `Show`.

Now, switch to the **Design** view and double-click on the **Show** button. This takes us into `Default.aspx.cs`. Delete the `Page_Load` block. We don't need that. The relevant portion of the starting code for this project should look like *Figure 12.7.1*:

```
1 //using is a directive
2 //System is a name space
3 //name space is a collection of features that our needs to run
4 using System;
5 //public means accessible anywhere
6 //partial means this class is split over multiple files
7 //class is a keyword and think of it as the outermost level of grouping
8 //:System.Web.UI.Page means our page inherits the features of a Page
9 public partial class _Default : System.Web.UI.Page
10 {
11     protected void Button1_Click(object sender, EventArgs e)
12     {
13
14     }
15 }
16
```

Figure 12.7.1: The starting code section for this project

In the next stage, go to the top of the file and, under `using System`, enter the following:

```
using System.Collections.Generic;
using System.Linq;
```

Creating an array

There is a lot of code to enter in this chapter, but it's mechanical. First, we will create an array, so enter the following between the curly braces under the line beginning with `protected void Button1_Click...`:

```
IEnumerable<int> scores = new int[] { 45, 98, 99, 78, 89, 87, 77, 67, 71, 81 };
```

Here, `IEnumerable` is the data type and `scores` is the name of the array. It doesn't matter what values you put into the array.

Averaging the values in a list

Now, first we will find an average of this list. So, enter the following next:

```
var goodStudentAverage = (from score in scores where score >= 90 select
score).Average();
```

We will select students who score 90 or above. Imagine, those are the semester grades for several students. So, in the preceding line, we're saying where the score is >=90, select that score. This is a query that you can write in a single line. In this context, score is the range variable, scores is the array, and the condition that selects is where score=>90. Then, you enter . (dot) Average() to average the whole thing out. In other words, the way that this is written is that the query between the parentheses will run and then average the list of values in the array. If you hover your mouse over var in this line, you'll see that it says double, because, as you can see if you hover your mouse over Average, it too returns a double. So, this Average() function acts on a list of the IEnumerable type, but it returns a double data type to us.

Displaying the results

Now, you can display the results, of course, because remember that it's just a single numerical value, an aggregation quantity. You can now say the following under this line:

```
sampLabel.Text = $"<br>The average for great students is
{goodStudentAverage}";
```

Using the Count function

Now, if you want, you can, for example, also use the Count function, so you could say something like the following next:

```
var averageStudentCount = scores.Where(grade =>70 <= grade && grade
<80).Count();
```

In the preceding line beginning with `var`, we used the query syntax in a single line, or inline query syntax, because we used `from` and `where`. Now, we can express the same thing using method chaining and the Lambda expressions within them. So, here we say `scores.Where`, and then we say where the `grade` is such that `70 <=grade`, but `grade <80`. Thus, we're defining people who earn scores of between `70` and `80`, exclusive of a score of `80`, and we're labeling them as average students. Then we'll `Count` those. This will tell us how many of these people are there and then we can display that number. For example, you can enter the following next:

```
sampLabel.Text += $"<br>There are {averageStudentCount} average students.";
```

Remember, `averageStudentCount` yields a number, so, for example, the results could be, *There are 25 average students.*

Working with a list of lists

Now, a very realistic application of this concept might be to have a list of lists. Start by entering the following next:

```
List<int> firstStudent = new List<int> { 90, 89, 92 };
```

Imagine that you have one student, `firstStudent`. Then, he or she has some grade scores, so you make `new List` of integers and then you initialize this list with some values within a set of curly braces. So, throw in some values as shown. (Note that the values I entered are in the `90` +/- range.) This is how you can initialize a list in away that we have not seen before.

Now, let's do one more list of integers for another student. To do this, enter the following for `secondStudent`, and write `new List` of integers. Again, initialize this list with another set of values. (Note, in this line, the values I will enter are in the `80` +/- range.) Now, when you have a whole class, you would have a list of such lists, correct? This works because you have multiple students to a class:

```
List<int> secondStudent = new List<int> { 78, 81, 79};
```

So, now you can create constructors. Enter the following next:

```
List<List<int>> classList = new List<List<int>>();
```

Adding students to the classList

Here, we have a list of lists of integers—you can embed lists inside other lists. Then, we will say, for example, the `classList` list, which equals a new list of lists. To initialize this list, you can use `Add`. For the next line, enter the following:

```
classList.Add(firstStudent);
classList.Add(secondStudent);
```

This is how you can add the first student, the second student, and so on to the class list.

Summarizing the information in the classList

In the next stage, you want to be able to get some useful information. For example, imagine you have this list of lists and you want to summarize. So, enter the following next:

```
var avgPerStudent = classList.Select(student => student.Average());
```

Now `avgPerStudent`, as an example, represents the average student grade. Now, after you type `classList.Select()`, the quantity to be selected is the list that represents each individual student, which is captured by `(student => student.Average())`. Now, be sure that you understand what a `student` parameter is. Here, you select a student and average out their grade scores. Hover your mouse over `student`, and as you can see, the quantity represents a list of integers that corresponds to the first student. Then, `student.Average` means averaging out that student and then repeating this process for the next student. If you hover your mouse over `var`, you'll see that the return in this case is of the `IEnumerable` type. You can iterate over those values. To do this, you'll enter the following next:

```
foreach(var studentAvg in avgPerStudent)
```

Now, underneath this line, enter the following within a set of curly braces to display the results:

```
sampLabel.Text += $"<br>Average grade={studentAvg}";
```

Running the program

Now, build this program and run it in your browser. Click on the **Show** button:

Figure 12.7.2: The results from running our program

Now these are some professional-looking results. The average for great students is **98.5**. There are three average students. The extended average grade for the two lists is shown at the end.

So, you learned more of what can be done with LINQ—the `Average` function and the `Count` function and you also learned that you can make a list of lists. You can operate on these lists using statements such as `Select` and then you can embed Lambda expressions to act on each list in the list of lists individually.

Chapter review

For review, the complete version of the `Default.aspx.cs` file for this chapter, including comments, is shown in the following code block:

```
//using is a directive
//System is a name space
//name space is a collection of features that our needs to run
using System;
using System.Collections.Generic;
using System.Linq;
//public means accessible anywhere
//partial means this class is split over multiple files
//class is a keyword and think of it as the outermost level of grouping
//:System.Web.UI.Page means our page inherits the features of a Page
public partial class _Default : System.Web.UI.Page
{
    protected void Button1_Click(object sender, EventArgs e)
    {
        IEnumerable<int> scores =
        new int[] { 45, 98, 99, 78, 89, 87, 77, 67, 71, 81 };
```

```
            //array of integers
            //line 17 below selects all scores 90 or above, and averages them,
            //giving back a double value
            var goodStudentAverage = (from score in scores where score >= 90
 select score).Average();
            //line 19 below displays the average
            sampLabel.Text = $"<br>The average for great students is
 {goodStudentAverage}";
            //line 21 below selects all students below 70 and 80,
            //and counts them
            var averageStudentCount = scores.Where(grade => 70 <= grade &&
 grade < 80).Count();
            //line 23 below displays the student count
            sampLabel.Text += $"<br>There are {averageStudentCount} average
 students.";
            //lines 25 and 26 create two new lists with initializer lists
            List<int> firstStudent = new List<int> {90,89,92};
            List<int> secondStudent = new List<int> { 78, 81, 79 };
            //line 28 creates a list of lists
            List<List<int>> classList = new List<List<int>>();
            classList.Add(firstStudent);
            classList.Add(secondStudent);
            //line 32 below find the average for each list, and
            //stores the averages
            //so avgPerStudent is of type IEnumerable
            var avgPerStudent = classList.Select(student => student.Average());
            //lines 35-38 display the averages
            foreach(var studentAvg in avgPerStudent)
            {
                sampLabel.Text += $"<br>Average grade={studentAvg}";
            }
        }
    }
```

Summary

In this chapter, we explored LINQ further. Specifically, we looked at the power of LINQ to perform aggregation functions, such as averaging, summation, and counting. Also, we talked about lists of lists. You averaged the values in a list, used the Count function, worked with a list of lists, added students to the classList, and summarized the information in the classList.

In the next chapter, you will learn about tuples, which are basically collections of several values.

13

Using LINQ to Summarize Tuples

In this chapter, you will learn about tuples. These are basically collections of several values.

Adding a show tuple summary values button to the HTML

Bring up a project and put in a button below the line beginning with `<form id=`.....
Replace the button text with `Show Tuple Summary Values`.

Now, switch to the **Design** view and double-click on the **Show Tuple Summary Values** button. This takes us into `Default.aspx.cs`. Delete the `Page_Load` block. The relevant portion of the starting code for this project should look like *Figure 13.8.1*:

```
1 //using is a directive
2 //System is a name space
3 //name space is a collection of features that our needs to run
4 using System;
5 //public means accessible anywhere
6 //partial means this class is split over multiple files
7 //class is a keyword and think of it as the outermost level of grouping
8 //:System.Web.UI.Page means our page inherits the features of a Page
9 public partial class _Default : System.Web.UI.Page
10 {
11
12     protected void Button1_Click(object sender, EventArgs e)
13     {
14
15     }
16 }
17
```

Figure 13.8.1: The starting code section for this project

Introducing tuples

Now, first we will make a function that returns tuple values. So, what is a tuple? Let's define them. As I said earlier, it's basically a collection of several values. Now, in C#, this means that you'll enter the following below the closed curly brace under the line that begins with `public partial class...`:

```
private static Tuple<double, double, double, double>
SummarizeList(List<double> listDoubles)
```

In the preceding line, `Tuple` is a class. Then, to define the number of values that the tuple stores, remember our work with vectors. We did two or three values to a vector. This is a similar concept. If you hover your mouse over `Tuple`, it says that *Tuple represents n-tuple* where *n* is eight or greater, so T1, T2, T3, up to TRest. Wow, so you can make eight or more tuples!

Adding namespaces

In our case, we put `<double, double, double, double>`. So, this is a tuple that can hold four values. Notice that as you type, `List<double>` is not showing, so you need to add some namespaces. Under `using System` at the top of the file, enter the following:

```
using System.Collections.Generic;
using System.Linq;
```

Here, we use generic collections and LINQ, and now `List<double>` shows up highlighted as it should be and we'll call it `listDoubles`.

Making a list with a tuple

In the next stage in the process, you'll make this list. So, enter the following between a set of curly braces below this line:

```
Tuple<double, double, double, double> summary =
Tuple.Create(listDoubles.Sum(),listDoubles.Average(),listDoubles.Max(),
listDoubles.Min());
```

To form the tuple, you say `Tuple.Create(listDoubles.Sum()`. `Tuple` is the name of the class, and one of the members inside this class is the `Create` function, so select it. Now, we can create a tuple with four entries. Next, we say `listDoubles.Sum()`. Notice that, when you type `Sum`, it's an extension method. If you remove `Sum`, you'll notice that `Linq` becomes grayed out. This again confirms why `Linq` is needed—for the `Sum` function.

The first entry in this tuple is the Sum of the list. Remember, we're calling `summary`. So, it would be like a statistical summary, so to speak, of the entries in the list. Beyond `listDoubles.Sum()` you can, of course, also have some other ones. You can have an average, `listDoubles.Average()`, and you can also add `listDoubles.Max()` and `listDoubles.Min()`.

Returning the tuples

At the end, you can return the tuples. To do this, enter the following below this line:

```
return summary;
```

In the first line you wrote earlier, remember `private` means accessible only there, `static` indicates that it runs on the class level, which means that you can call `SummarizeList` directly with a name—you don't need an object to put it on.

Now, in this particular case, it will return this construct, `Tuple<double, double, double, double>`, known as a tuple, which here is just a way of storing four double values. Then, to create a tuple for the first entry, you use LINQ. Then you use LINQ for the second entry, LINQ for the third entry, and finally, LINQ for the fourth entry. So, `Sum`, `Min`, `Max`, and `Average` are extension methods and then you `return` it.

Making a list of doubles

Now, for the next stage, take a look at the Button click event. This code here is quite straightforward. Start by entering the following within the set of curly braces under the line that begins with `protected void Button1_Click....` You will make a list of doubles, called `lst`, as shown here:

```
List<double> lst = new List<double> { 1, 2, 5, 68, 899, 1, -989, 0.1143,
98, 2553 };
```

After the `new List of double` values, you specify the initializer between curly braces by throwing in some numbers—it doesn't matter what they are, right? Put in some negatives, some decimals, some integers, and so on.

Summarizing the list

Next, we will call `SummarizeList`. So, enter the following below this line:

```
var results = SummarizeList(lst);
```

In this case, to be honest, `var` is easy, right? If you don't use that, you'll have to type `Tuple<double, double, double, double>`, which would be the data type. That's really long-winded, in other words, and it takes a lot of space. So, remember, `var` signifies implicit data typing but it is smart enough to know what the data type is.

Displaying the results

Then once you return it, you can go to the item store there. So, you can enter the following next:

```
sampLabel.Text = $"Sum={results.Item1}";
```

In the next stage, copy this line and paste it in directly below it. Edit the text for the `Average` function to read as follows:

```
sampLabel.Text += $"<br>Average={results.Item2}";
```

Make sure that the way you call these lines correspond to the functions; so, `Sum`, `Average`, `Max`, and `Min`. Again, copy the preceding line and paste it directly below, so you don't have to append. Since the next one is for `Max`, edit the text to read as follows:

```
sampLabel.Text += $"<br>Max={results.Item3}";
```

This will be `Item3` and the tuple that you can extract.

Finally, let's do one more. So again, copy the preceding line and paste it directly below. Since the last one is for `Min`, edit the text to read as follows:

```
sampLabel.Text += $"<br>Min={results.Item4}";
```

This, of course, is `Item4` and the tuple that you can extract.

Running the program

Now, let's crank it up in your browser. Click on the **Show Tuple Summary Values** button. The results are shown in *Figure 13.8.2*:

Figure 13.8.2: The results of running our program for this chapter

You see **Sum**, **Average**, **Max**, and **Min**, so it's working as expected.

Now, as a more realistic extension of this, imagine a list of tuples. You can definitely do that, so you can add something like this below the last line:

```
List<Tuple<string, double, double, decimal>>;
```

You can have a list of Tuples. Each Tuple represents, for example, information about a person, and then you would have a list of people. This is something for you to think about: how to construct it and make a project out of it for yourself. However, these are the fundamentals here.

Chapter review

For review, the complete version of the `Default.aspx.cs` for this chapter, including comments, is shown in the following code block:

```
//using is a directive
//System is a name space
//name space is a collection of features that our needs to run
using System;
using System.Collections.Generic;
using System.Linq;
//public means accessible anywhere
//partial means this class is split over multiple files
//class is a keyword and think of it as the outermost level of grouping
//:System.Web.UI.Page means our page inherits the features of a Page
public partial class _Default : System.Web.UI.Page
{
    private static Tuple<double, double, double , double>
```

```
SummarizeList(List<double> listDoubles)
    {
        Tuple<double, double, double, double> summary =
        Tuple.Create(listDoubles.Sum(),
        listDoubles.Average(), listDoubles.Max(), listDoubles.Min());
    return summary;
    }
    protected void Button1_Click(object sender, EventArgs e)
    {
        List<double> lst =
        new List<double> { 1, 2, 5, 68, 899, 1, -989, 0.1143, 98, 2553 };
        var results = SummarizeList(lst);
        sampLabel.Text = $"Sum={results.Item1}";
        sampLabel.Text += $"<br>Average={results.Item2}";
        sampLabel.Text += $"<br>Max={results.Item3}";
        sampLabel.Text += $"<br>Min={results.Item4}";
    }
}
```

Summary

In this chapter, you learned about tuples, which are basically collections of several values. You made a list with a tuple, returned tuples, and summarized a list.

In the next chapter, we will talk about using LINQ to group related results. Grouping is a fundamental thing that you do in databases to categorize results.

14
Summarizing Results with Grouping

In this chapter, we will talk about using LINQ to group related results. Grouping is a fundamental thing that you do in databases to categorize results.

Adding a Show Results button to the HTML

Bring up a project. First, we will put a button in the HTML that says **Show Results**; to do this, place a button below the line beginning with `<form id=....`:

```
<asp:Button ID="Button1" runat="server" Text="Show Results" /><br />
```

Next, switch to the **Design** view and double-click on the **Show Results** button. This takes us into `Default.aspx.cs`. Delete the `Page_Load` block. The relevant portion of the starting code for this project should look like *Figure 14.9.1*:

```
 1 //using is a directive
 2 //System is a name space
 3 //name space is a collection of features that our needs to run
 4 using System;
 5 //public means accessible anywhere
 6 //partial means this class is split over multiple files
 7 //class is a keyword and think of it as the outermost level of grouping
 8 //:System.Web.UI.Page means our page inherits the features of a Page
 9 public partial class _Default : System.Web.UI.Page
10 {
11     protected void Button1_Click(object sender, EventArgs e)
12     {
13
14     }
15 }
16
```

Figure 14.9.1: The starting code section for this project

Adding namespaces

First, we need to add a couple of namespaces. To do this, enter the following under `using System` near the top of the file:

```
using System.Linq;
using System.Collections.Generic;
```

Creating the student class and defining fields

Next, we will make a class called `Student`. Above the line beginning with `public partial class _Default...`, enter the following:

```
public class Student
```

Next, to define fields, enter the following between a set of curly braces below this line:

```
public string Name { get; set; }
```

So, little properties here, and then let's add one more. Enter the following below this line:

```
public List<int> Grades;
```

Here, `List<int>` is for the grades of the students, and let's name it `Grades`.

Making a list of students

Now, in the next stage, we will make a list of students. To do this, start by entering the following between the set of curly braces after the line that begins with `protected void Button1_Click...`:

```
List<Student> students = new List<Student>
```

Here, `students` is the name of the list. We then have a new list of students. Next, to initialize the list, we'll place all of the new students between a set of curly braces below this line, starting as follows:

```
new Student {Name="Smith, John", Grades=new List<int> {78,98,67,87 } },
```

In the preceding line, after `new Student`, you place all of the information for each student individually within a set of curly braces. First, you need to define the value of `Name`, so you set that equal to `Smith, John` for example, insert a comma and then put in `Grades` of John in a new list of integers, setting those values to 78, 98, 67, and 87.

Next, we need to repeat this a couple of times for other the students; so, copy this line and paste it below. Edit the line to change the value of `Name` variable to `Adams, Amy`, and the grades to 91,99,89, and 93:

```
new Student {Name="Adams, Amy", Grades=new List<int> {91,99,89,93 } },
```

 This level of coding is very practical and realistic. Having done coding for five years, I can tell you that things are always far more interesting and more challenging.

Now, repeat this process one more time. Copy the preceding line and paste it below. Edit the line to change the value of `Name` variable to `Smith, Mary`, and the grades to 89, 87, 84, and 88. Be sure to insert a closed curly brace and a semicolon on the next line following the last `new Student` class:

```
new Student {Name="Smith, Mary", Grades=new List<int> {89,87,84,88 }};
```

Grouping names

Again, because we want to group, for example, by the last name and the first name, that's why I have used two identical last names. We will display the results nicely grouped by the last name; that is, by the first letter of the last name and then by the first name.

Next, we will write our LINQ query to accomplish the grouping. Again, this could be done in a much more sophisticated way, but is a relatively easy example. So, below the closed curly brace and semicolon on the line following the last `new Student` class in the list, enter the following:

```
var groupsByFirstLetters = from student in students group student by
student.Name[0];
```

Remember, `groupsByFirstLetters` indicates the first letter of the last name. So, to write the query, you say `fromstudent` in `students`, and then on the next line you `group` students by `student.Name`. Because `Name` is a string, you can extract the first character by using square brackets and then getting the value at index 0 in the string. That's why you can write that. Otherwise, it would seem a little mysterious.

Displaying the grouped results

Now, to display the results in a grouped fashion, you have to use nested `foreach` loops. So, enter the following next:

```
foreach(var studentGroup in groupsByFirstLetters)
```

Here, it gets a little more interesting. If you hover your mouse over `var` momentarily, it tells you what `var` represents. It says, *it's a Grouping of characters and students. It represents a collection of objects that have a common key.*

Now, we can make use of it as follows. Enter the following between a set of curly braces underneath the preceding line:

```
sampLabel.Text += $"<br>{studentGroup.Key}";
```

First we want to display the key, meaning the first letter of each last name, and then everything will be summarized under the first letter of that last name. So, we say `studentGroup.Key`. There's a property called `Key`, which is the key to the grouping, for each group. Remember that here we are grouping by the first letter of the last name. So, the key is that quantity.

Next, once you fix the first letter within that group, there are several students usually or several items, correct? So, now you have to display those items individually. Enter the following next:

```
foreach(var st in studentGroup)
```

Notice something here about the nesting of the `foreach` loops. Do you see how in the `foreach (var studentGroup in groupsByFirstLetters)` line, the outer `for` loop gets the `studentGroup` variable, and then the key of that group is displayed by the `sampLabel.Text += $"<br>{studentGroup.Key}"` line? Well, next you'll go through the students inside of each of these groups. That's why in the next stage, if you hover your mouse over `var` in the preceding line, you see that it says, `student st in studentGroup`. So, that's the breakdown.

Next, to display it, enter the following within a set of curly braces under the preceding `foreach` line:

```
sampLabel.Text += $"<br>{st.Name}";
```

This is the heart of it. Now remember, we started with a class called `Student`. Then we have a list of students. Note that in the list of students, you can also use a syntax that says name of the property and then the value of property without the parentheses. You can just use curly braces to make the objects directly inside the definition of the list of students.

The block beginning with `var groupsByFirstLetters...` groups things for us. Then we need that outer loop, `foreach (var studentGroup...`, to display the key to each group. Then the inner `foreach` loop, `foreach (var st in studentGroup)`, displays the students within that group. So, the two loops are needed, and they serve different purposes.

Now crank this up in your browser, and take a look at the results. Click on the **Show Results** button. As you can see, in *Figure 14.9.2*, you have the letter **S**, which is the key for the first group and within that group you have **Smith, John** and then **Smith, Mary**. Next, you have the letter **A**, which is the key for the second group, and within that you have **Adams, Amy**:

Figure 14.9.2: The results of running the program for this chapter

Of course, this can be sorted and all kinds of other things can be done. However, these are just the basics. So, you see what is doable here; many much more sophisticated things are possible.

Chapter review

For review, the complete version of the `Default.aspx.cs` file for this chapter, including comments, is shown in the following code block:

```
//using is a directive
//System is a name space
//name space is a collection of features that our needs to run
using System;
using System.Linq;
using System.Collections.Generic;
//public means accessible anywhere
//partial means this class is split over multiple files
//class is a keyword and think of it as the outermost level of grouping
//:System.Web.UI.Page means our page inherits the features of a Page
public class Student //define student class
{
    public string Name { get; set; }
    public List<int> Grades;
}
public partial class _Default : System.Web.UI.Page
{
    protected void Button1_Click(object sender, EventArgs e)
    {
        //create list of students
        List<Student> students = new List<Student>
        {
            new Student {Name="Smith, John",
            Grades=new List<int> {78,98,67,87}},
            new Student {Name="Adams, Amy",
            Grades=new List<int> {91,99,89,93}},
            new Student {Name="Smith, Mary",
            Grades=new List<int> {89,87,84,88}}
        };
        //create query that groups students by first letter of last name
        //Name is a string, so student.Name[0] means grab the
        //first character for grouping
        var groupsByFirstLetters =
        from student in students group student by student.Name[0];
        //the outer loop is needed to display the "Key",
        //which is the first letter for each group
```

```
        foreach(var studentGroup in groupsByFirstLetters)
        {
            sampLabel.Text += $"<br>{studentGroup.Key}";
            //the inner loop is needed to display the students
            //within each group
            foreach(var st in studentGroup)
            {
                sampLabel.Text += $"<br>{st.Name}";
            }
        }
    }
}
```

Summary

In this chapter, we talked about using LINQ to group related results. You created a student class and defined fields, made a list of students, grouped names, and finally, displayed the grouped results.

In the next chapter, you will learn how to use LINQ to write queries that join different result sets or different data sets.

15

Joining Datasets with Inner Joins

In this chapter, you will learn how to use LINQ to write queries that join different result sets or different data sets. The code is not very complicated in this chapter—there's just a bit of it.

Adding a Join Classes button to the HTML

Bring up a project. Put a button in the HTML page that says **Join Classes** below the line beginning with `<form id=`.... So, we'll have two different classes and then we'll join them together, produce some results, and then display them. That's the objective here:

```
<asp:Button ID="Button1" runat="server" Text="Join Classes" />
```

Next, switch to the **Design** view and double-click on the **Join Classes** button. This takes us into `Default.aspx.cs`. Delete the `Page_Load` block. The relevant portion of the starting code for this project should look like *Figure 15.10.1*:

```
1 //using is a directive
2 //System is a name space
3 //name space is a collection of features that our needs to run
4 using System;
5 //public means accessible anywhere
6 //partial means this class is split over multiple files
7 //class is a keyword and think of it as the outermost level of grouping
8 //:System.Web.UI.Page means our page inherits the features of a Page
9 public partial class _Default : System.Web.UI.Page
10 {
11     protected void Button1_Click(object sender, EventArgs e)
12     {
13
14     }
15 }
16
```

Figure 15.10.1: The starting code section for this project

Adding the namespaces

Now, we will make code as follows. We'll need the LINQ and generic collections namespaces; so, enter the following under `using System` near the top of the file:

```
using System.Linq;
using System.Collections.Generic;
```

Creating the person and car classes

We'll make two classes. One will be a `person` and the other will be a `car` class. To do this, enter the following directly above the line that begins with `public partial class _Default...`:

```
public class Person
```

Now, we need just a name; so, enter the following between a set of curly braces below this line:

```
public string Name { get; set; }
```

Then, we also need to make a class called `Car`. So, beneath the closed curly brace underneath the preceding line, enter the following:

```
public class Car
```

Next, enter the following between a set of curly braces below this line:

```
public Person Owner { get; set; }
```

As you can see now, `public Person` is being defined inside the class as a data type of a field. For example, a car has an owner.

Now, add one more data type below the preceding line, as follows:

```
public string Maker { get; set; }
```

Clearly, you can see the presence of the `Person` field inside the `Car` class. There's a connection between the classes. We will use this shortly. For now, let's go through the construction.

Making person objects

First, we have to make some `Person` objects, otherwise we won't have anything to join. So, enter the following between a set of curly braces under the line that begins with `protected void Button1_Click...`:

```
Person per1 = new Person() { Name = "Mark Owens" };
```

Now, copy this line and paste it directly below. Edit the line to say `Person per2` and change the value of `Name` variable to equal `Jenny Smith`:

```
Person per2 = new Person() { Name = "Jenny Smith" };
```

Finally, copy the preceding line and paste it below. Edit the line to say `Person per3` and change the value of `Name` variable to equal `John Jenkins`:

```
Person per3 = new Person() { Name = "John Jenkins" };
```

So, now we have some people who will be the car owners.

Making car objects

Now, let's make some `car` objects. Skip a line and then start by entering the following:

```
Car car1 = new Car() { Owner = per1, Maker = "Honda" };
```

To initialize `car1`, you start by saying `Owner = per1`. This establishes a connection between the two classes; that is, owner for `car1` is `per1`, who is `Mark Owens`. Then, you add maker, which we'll say is `Honda` for `car1`.

Once again, copy this line and paste it directly below the preceding line. Edit the line to say `Car car2` and owner to say `per2`, but leave maker equal to `Honda`:

```
Car car2 = new Car() { Owner = per2, Maker = "Honda" };
```

Sometimes, unfortunately, to illustrate a concept, I've got to write a decent amount of code, otherwise the concept is difficult to illustrate.

Again, copy the preceding line and paste it below. Edit the line to say `Car car3` and `Owner` to say `per1`, but this time and change `Maker` equal to `Toyota`:

```
Car car3 = new Car() { Owner = per1, Maker = "Toyota" };
```

Finally, copy the preceding line and paste it below. Edit the line to say `Car car4`, `Owner` to say `per4` and `Maker` equal to `Tesla`:

```
Car car4 = new Car() { Owner = per2, Maker = "Tesla" };
```

The thing to be observed here, of course, is that the `per3` variable is not being used as the owner of a car, right? So, when we do the join, the query that joins these two datasets, the records that are shared will be returned. This means, for example, that there is no car owned by `per3`.

Making a list of owners and their cars

Next, skip a line and enter the following:

```
List<Person> people = new List<Person> { per1, per2, per3 };
```

Here, we are saying a list of persons, `people`, equals a new list of people and, then, we stick in those individuals—`per1`, `per2`, and `per3`. Next, you'll do the same thing for the cars, so enter the following:

```
List<Car> cars = new List<Car> { car1, car2, car3, car4 };
```

Again, to initialize the list of cars, you say `car1`, `car2`, `car3`, and `car4`.

Joining the owners and car lists

Now, you can join those lists. To do this, skip a line, and enter the following next:

```
var carsWithOwners = from person in people
```

For cars with owners, you write the query: `from person in people`. Next, continue by entering the following below:

```
join car in cars on person equals car.Owner
```

Here, we are joining the two lists. We are using `person` to `join people` and setting that equal to `car.Owner`. Then, once you have them joined, the people who have a car essentially, you can say the following next:

```
select new{ OwnerName = person.Name, CarMake = car.Maker };
```

We are creating an anonymous type in this line. So, if you hover your mouse over `var`, it says **T is 'a**. That's an anonymous data type. So, `carsWithOwners` is basically a list of anonymous types, but because it is a list and because it is `IEnumerable`, you can step through it using a `foreach` loop.

Getting and displaying the results

Now we need to get the results. So, skip a line, and say the following:

```
foreach(var ownedCar in carsWithOwners)
```

Next, enter the following between a set of curly braces below this line:

```
sampLabel.Text += $"<br>Owner={ownedCar.OwnerName} Car
Make={ownedCar.CarMake}";
```

This will display the results for us.

Running the program

Now open this up in your browser, and click on the **Join Classes** button. Take a look at the results, which are also shown in *Figure 15.10.2*:

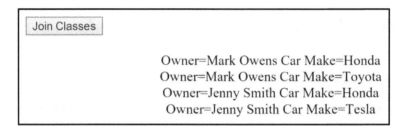

Figure 15.10.2: The result of this project

So, Mark Owens has two cars. Next, Jenny Smith has a Honda and also a Tesla. Correct?

Now, because John Jenkins is `per3`, he does not appear as an owner in the list of cars. This means that there's no connection between `per3` and the `Car` list. In other words, when the join is done in LINQ, `per1` is used because it is going by the owner—`Car.Owner`. So, `per1` and `per2` will be used, but not `per3`. Then, you display the results.

Chapter review

For review, the complete version of the `Default.aspx.cs` file for this chapter, including comments, is shown in the following code block:

```
//using is a directive
//System is a name space
//name space is a collection of features that our needs to run
using System;
using System.Linq;
using System.Collections.Generic;
//public means accessible anywhere
//partial means this class is split over multiple files
//class is a keyword and think of it as the outermost level of grouping
//:System.Web.UI.Page means our page inherits the features of a Page
public class Person
{
    //define Person class
    public string Name { get; set; }
}
public class Car
```

```
{
    //define Car class, using field of type Person
    public Person Owner { get; set; }
    public string Maker { get; set; }
}
public partial class _Default : System.Web.UI.Page
{
    protected void Button1_Click(object sender, EventArgs e)
    {
        //make three new people
        Person per1 = new Person() { Name = "Mark Owens" };
        Person per2 = new Person() { Name = "Jenny Smith" };
        Person per3 = new Person() { Name = "John Jenkins" };
        //make four new cars
        Car car1 = new Car() { Owner = per1, Maker = "Honda" };
        Car car2 = new Car() { Owner = per2, Maker = "Honda" };
        Car car3 = new Car() { Owner = per1, Maker = "Toyota" };
        Car car4 = new Car() { Owner = per2, Maker = "Tesla" };
        //make lists of people and cars
        List<Person> people = new List<Person> { per1, per2, per3 };
        List<Car> cars = new List<Car> { car1, car2, car3, car4 };
        //use linq to write a query that joins the two lists by car Owner
        //here, the type of var is an enumerable list of anonymous
        //data types
        var carsWithOwners = from person in people join car in cars on
person equals car.Owner
        select new { OwnerName = person.Name, CarMake = car.Maker };
        //foreach loops iterates over carsWithOwners
        foreach(var ownedCar in carsWithOwners)
        {
            sampLabel.Text += $"<br>Owner={ownedCar.OwnerName} Car Make=
{ownedCar.CarMake}";
        }
    }
}
```

Summary

In this chapter, you learned how to use LINQ to write queries that join different result sets or different data sets. You created the `Person` and `Car` classes, made the `Person` and `Car` objects, made a list of owners and their cars, and joined the owners and car lists.

In the next chapter, you will work with SQL Server 2017 Express.

16

Downloading, Installing, and Running SQL Server 2017

In this chapter, you will download, install, and run SQL Server 2017 Express.

Downloading SQL Server 2017 express

Click on the following link to bring you to the site where you can download SQL Server 2017 Express, as shown in *Figure 16.1.1*:

```
https://www.microsoft.com/en-us/sql-server/sql-server-editions-express
```

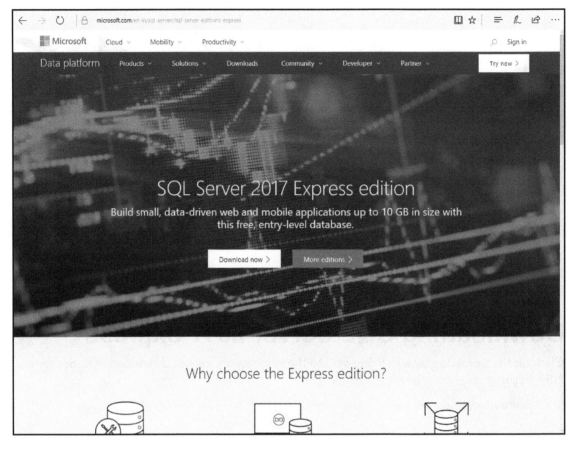

Figure 16.1.1: Download screen for SQL Server 2017 Express edition

Next, click on the **Download now** button. When the download is complete, double-click on `SQL Server2017-SSEI-Expr.exe`. Answer **Yes** on the **User Account Control** screen.

Selecting the installation type

Next, you will need to select the installation type, as shown in *Figure 16.1.2*. Choose **Basic installation** and accept the **License Terms agreement**:

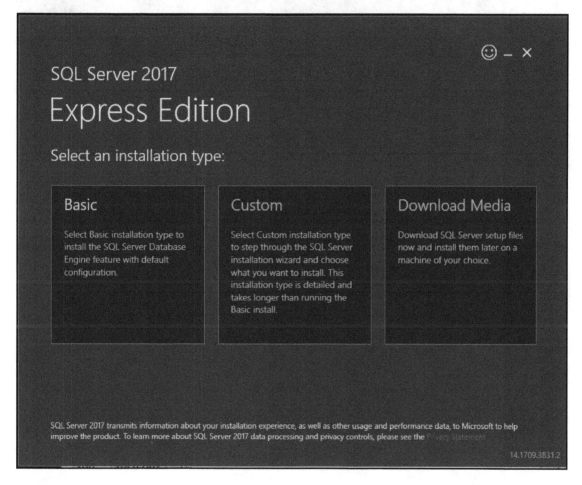

Figure 16.1.2: Select the Basic installation from the installation type screen

Installing the package

Next, either accept the default install location or choose one of your own. The install package will then download and install the program. Be patient during the installation process, as it is a big program and it might take a little while.

When the installation has completed, you will see a screen similar to the one shown in *Figure 16.1.3*:

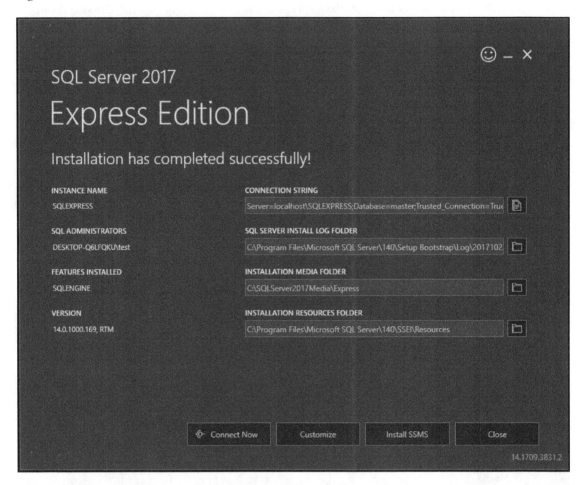

Figure 16.1.3: The installation has completed successfully

Working with SQL server inside Visual Studio

Once we have SQL server downloaded and installed, let's take a look at it inside Visual Studio. Go to **View** and then select **SQL Server Object Explorer**; it opens a little pane on the left-hand side, as shown in *Figure 16.1.4*:

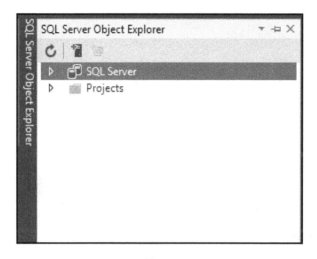

Figure 16.1.4: The SQL Server Object Explorer pane in Visual Studio

Next, click on the **Add SQL Server** Button, as shown in *Figure 16.1.5*:

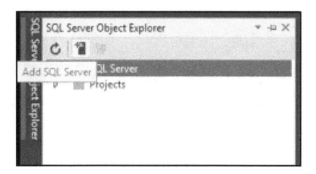

Figure 16.1.5: The Add SQL Server Button

Now, the dialog box shown in *Figure 16.1.6* appears. Notice where it says **Windows Authentication.** This is known as *integrated security*. You don't have to specify a different username and password. Just fill the **Server Name** field, click on **Connect**, and you'll be logged in to it:

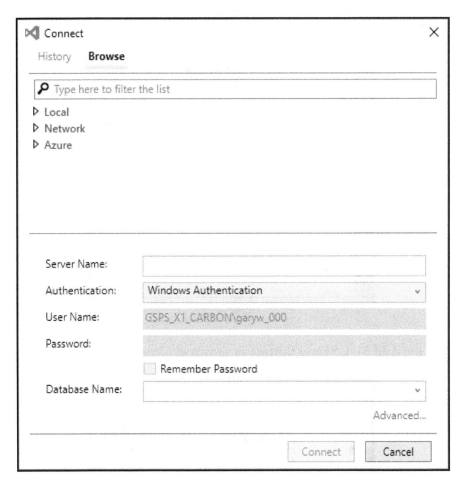

Figure 16.1.6: The Connect dialog box

The specific version that you have will be different than the one shown in *Figure 16.1.7*, but these are the basic things that will apply to many different versions:

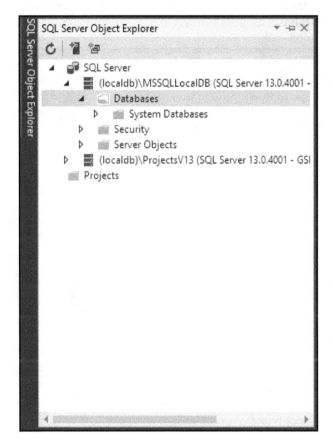

Figure 16.1.7: The Databases folder specific to this version of SQL Server 2017 Express

Creating a SQL server database

Now, we will create a database. To do this, expand the **Databases** folder and right-click on it. Select **Add New Database**, as shown in *Figure 16.1.8*, and name the database People:

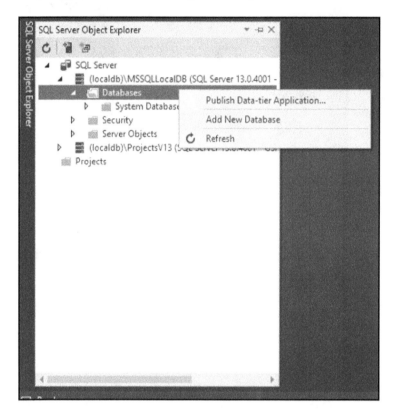

Figure 16.1.8: Adding a new database

Adding and defining a table

Now, expand the **People** node and then, within that, you will see a folder called **Tables**. Again, expand the **Tables** node, as you have to add your own table. Your **SQL Server Object Explorer** pane should look like the one shown in *Figure 16.1.9*:

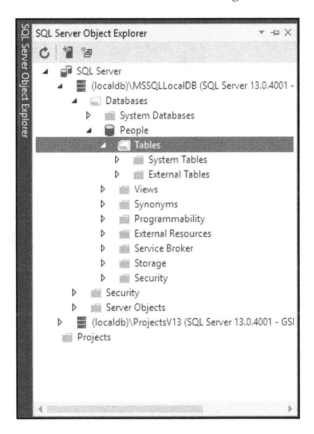

Figure 16.1.9: The SQL Server Object Explorer pane with the People node and the Tables node expanded

Now, right-click on the **Tables** folder and select **Add New Table**. This brings up the table definition stage, which is shown in *Figure 16.1.10*:

Figure 16.1.10: Table Definition screen

This is where you define the table. Look at the first field with a little key, which appears near the top-left in the screenshot. This key would be used to identify the records or the rows of the table, and further, when you want to have auto generation enabled. In other words, you want the number assigned to each record to be generated automatically, so that you don't have to keep track of it.

So, if you right-click on the key and select **Properties**, it brings up the panel, shown in *Figure 16.1.11*, on the right-hand side of the screen:

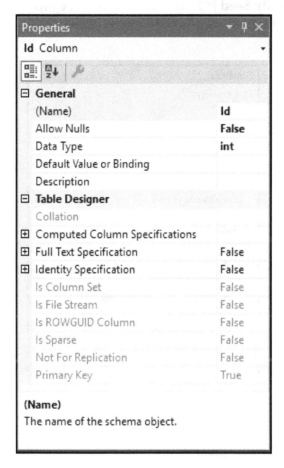

Figure 16.1.11: The Table properties panel

Now, look where it says **Identity Specification**. Expand that node and then, where it says **Is Identity**, choose **True** from the dropdown. As can be seen in *Figure 16.1.12*, **Identity Increment** is **1** and **Identity Seed** is **1**, which is fine. So, it begins at **1** and every time a new record is added, the record number grows by 1 only. Notice that it also automatically changes the Code view.

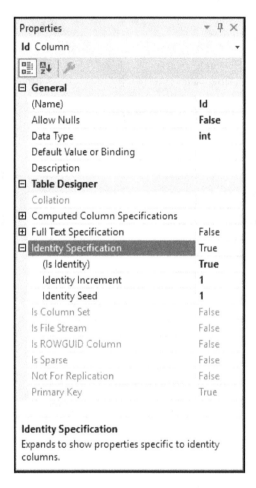

Figure 16.1.12: Setting the Identity Specification

Now, in the **T-SQL** window at the bottom of the screen, it says CREATE TABLE [dbo].[Table]. If you change [Table] to say [People], that's now the table name, as shown in *Figure 16.1.13*:

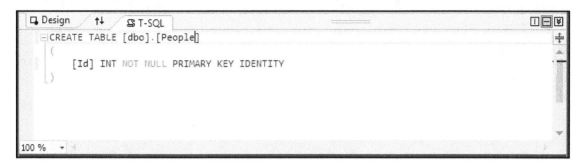

Figure 16.1.13: Changing the Name of the table

In the following line, [Id] is the name of a column or a field; INT is the data type, NOT NULL means that entries must be specified, and PRIMARY KEY is used to identify records; you know what IDENTITY is by now, as you've seen it in previous steps.

Adding fields to the table

Now, you'll add your own fields and your own columns. So next, enter the following:

```
[NAME] VARCHAR(100) NOT NULL
```

This is the NAME field, and the data type is varchar, which stands for variable character. This is basically a text field, so specify the length as 100, and because the entry should be specified, we will make it NOT NULL.

Let's add one more field. To do this, enter the following next:

```
[DATEADDED] DATE NULL
```

Here, DATE ADDED is the date on which the record is added and DATE is the data type. Your screen should look like the one shown in *Figure 16.1.14*.

Again, if you don't want nulls, you can uncheck these in the **Design** window. So, the Table view in **Design** tab and the Code view interact:

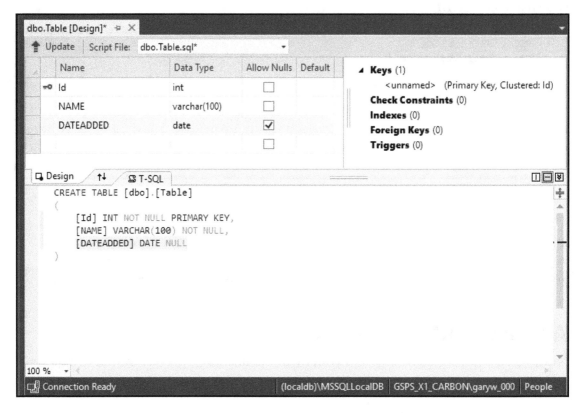

Figure 16.1.14: Two fields, NAME and DATEADDED, have been added to the table

Here, one thing to note is where it says **T-SQL** on the tab. Well, SQL is *Structured Query Language* and the Microsoft version is T-SQL or *Transact Structured Query Language*. The core is pretty much the same, but there are some additions in the Microsoft version.

Updating the structure of the database

Now you have to update the structure of things, so click on the **Update** button in the upper-right corner of the screen. Give it a second to update everything and then click on the **Update Database** button.

As seen in *Figure 16.1.15*, the update completed successfully:

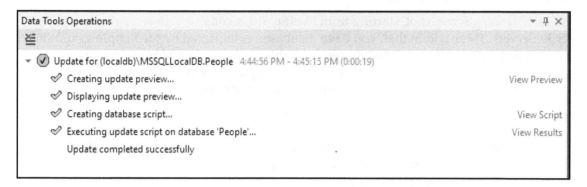

Figure 16.1.15: The database update is complete and successful!

Now, in the **SQL Server Object Explorer** pane on the left-hand side, if you expand **dbo.People** and then expand **Columns**, you can see the default field or column and the new ones you created, as shown in *Figure 16.1.16*:

Figure 16.1.16: The columns we created in dbo.People

Chapter review

In the preceding screenshot, starting from the top, the second item down indicates a server (SQL Server). Then, within that, you have databases as indicated by the **People** icon. When you expand a database, you have an icon for **Tables**, an icon for **Columns**, and the key icon that indicates the primary key. So, there is a meaning to the little icons that are used. They represent different levels of nesting within this database structure.

These are the basics.

So, be sure that you can re-create all of this. Exit out of this window, and now, click on **View** and go to **Start Page**. Then, do the following:

1. Open the **SQL Server Object Explorer** pane.
2. Right click on **SQL Server**.
3. Select **Disconnect** from the drop-down menu.
4. Right-click again, and select **Add SQL Server** from the drop-down menu.
5. Browse for your server.
6. Click on the **Connect** button at the bottom of the **Connect** screen.
7. Expand the server to show the Databases folder.
8. Expand the Databases folder, and there you can see the People database.
9. Open the Tables folder, and there's the dbo.People table.

Summary

In this chapter, you downloaded, installed, and ran SQL Server 2017 Express. You worked with SQL Server within Visual Studio, connecting the two, created a SQL Server database, added and defined a table, added fields to the table, and updated the structure of the database.

In the next chapter, you will learn how to connect to SQL Server and then display the records from the database table in a web page.

17

Writing Code to Manually Connect to a Table and Retrieve Records

In this chapter, you will learn how to connect to SQL Server and then display the records from a database table, `dbo.People`, in a web page.

Adding a show records button to the HTML

Bring up a project and, into the **<html>** page, we place a button below the line beginning with `<form id=`..... For this, go to **Toolbox**, grab a `Button` control, and drag it in there. Change the text on the button to say `Show Records`. Remember, a *record* is just one row of information and a row, of course, is a line in a table, for example, that goes across from left to right.

Now, switch to the **Design** view, and left double-click the **Show Records** button. This takes us into `Default.aspx.cs` with the event handler. Delete the `Page_Load` block. The relevant portion of the starting code for this project should look like *Figure 17.2.1*:

```
1    //using is a directive
2    //System is a name space
3    //name space is a collection of features that our needs to run
4    using System;
5                            //public means accessible anywhere
6                            //partial means this class is split over multiple files
7                            //class is a keyword and think of it as the outermost level of grouping
8                            //:System.Web.UI.Page means our page inherits the features of a Page
9    public partial class _Default : System.Web.UI.Page
10   {
11       protected void Button1_Click(object sender, EventArgs e)
12       {
13
14       }
15   }
16
```

Figure 17.2.1: The starting code section for this project

Adding a namespace

To make this work with SQL Server, you have to add a namespace. So, go to the top of the file, and; enter the following under `using System`:

```
using System.Data.SqlClient;
```

Making the connection string

Now, beyond this, we'll go through the construction of the code line-by-line. The first thing that you need is a *connection string*. So, let's do the following:

1. Open **SQL Server Object Explorer**.
2. Right-click on the name of your database, in this case **People**, and view its **Properties**.
3. Then, to get the connection string, make sure that you expand the node called **General** within the **Properties** pane, and then go to the one that says **Connection string** and double-click on it to select it with its long description.

4. Next, right-click on the long description and copy it. (It's difficult to construct accurately by hand, so it's better just to copy it from there). This procedure is shown in *Figure 17.2.2*:

Figure 17.2.2: Copying the connection string

5. Now, enter the following within the set of curly braces beneath the line that begins with `protected void Button1_Click`...:

```
string connString = @"Data Source=(localdb)\MSSQLLocalDB;Initial
Catalog=People;Integrated Security=True;Connect
Timeout=30;Encrypt=False;TrustServerCertificate=True;ApplicationIntent=Read
Write;MultiSubnetFailover=False";
```

Here, after you enter `string connString =`, you put the @ symbol to indicate that it's a literal string or a verbatim string, which should be interpreted exactly as it looks. Then, you put the " " symbols and paste the long string between them. So, within this line of course, you have the `Data Source`, the name of the computer, `Initial Catalog` as the database, `Integrated Security` is `True` because we set it up that way, and some other pieces of information that aren't very important right now.

Connecting to SQL Server

To connect to SQL Server through the page, we will try the following. First, you have to create a command to be issued to SQL Server. To do this, enter the following next:

```
string commandText = "Select * from dbo.People";
```

Here, `Select  *` means to select all from `dbo.People`. Remember that we called our database `People`; so, this means select everything from the table in the `People` database. This is what it's saying: select everything from that table.

Now, one more thing. When you deal with low-level resources, especially reading hard drives, for example, you have to establish a channel of communication to the hard drive. So, because that is the case, type the following next:

```
using (SqlConnection conn = new SqlConnection(connString))
```

Here, `using` is a nice construct because it allows you to get a resource, use the resource, and then it disposes the resource for you—very nicely and very cleanly. For example, `SqlConnection` is such a thing.

Now, if you right-click on `SqlConnection` and select **Go to Definition** from the menu, and scroll to the bottom, you will see that there's a line that says, **Dispose-protected override void Dispose**. Now, if you expand the `protected override void Open()` line, it says, **Opens a database connection with the property settings specified by the system.Data.SqlClient.SqlConnection.ConnectionString**, as shown in *Figure 17.2.3*:

```
378      ...public SqlCommand CreateCommand();
386      ...public void EnlistDistributedTransaction(ITransaction transaction);
395      ...public override void EnlistTransaction(System.Transactions.Transaction transaction);
403      ...public override DataTable GetSchema();
411      ...public override DataTable GetSchema(string collectionName);
427      ...public override DataTable GetSchema(string collectionName, string[] restrictionValues);
447      //
448      // Summary:
449      //     Opens a database connection with the property settings specified by the
         System.Data.SqlClient.SqlConnection.ConnectionString.
450      //
451      // Exceptions:
452      //   T:System.InvalidOperationException:
453      //     Cannot open a connection without specifying a data source or server.orThe connection
454      //     is already open.
455      //
456      //   T:System.Data.SqlClient.SqlException:
457      //     A connection-level error occurred while opening the connection. If the
         System.Data.SqlClient.SqlException.Number
458      //     property contains the value 18487 or 18488, this indicates that the specified
459      //     password has expired or must be reset. See the System.Data.SqlClient.SqlConnection.ChangePassword
         (System.String,System.String)
460      //     method for more information.The <system.data.localdb> tag in the app.config file
461      //     has invalid or unknown elements.
462      //
```

Figure 17.2.3: Expanded definition for protected override void Open

If you ever want to know which exceptions could be thrown, everything is listed in the definition for `protected override void Open()` and likewise with `protected override void Close()`.

The constructors are the first ones listed in the definition. So, let's close this now.

Catching exceptions

In the next stage, because errors could be thrown, we'll use `try` and `catch`, so that we can catch them and display them to the user. Start by entering `try` on a line by itself below the open curly brace under the line that begins with `using (SqlConnection conn...`:

```
try
```

Next, insert a set of curly braces below `try`, and then underneath the closing curly brace there, enter the following:

```
catch (Exception ex)
```

Displaying errors

Now, if an error is generated, we will display it; so enter the following between a set of curly braces below this line:

```
sampLabel.Text = $"{ex.Message}";
```

A message that is useful will be displayed if something's wrong with the database connection.

Opening the connection

Let's continue with the connection now. First, let's try to open it. Enter the following between a set of curly braces under `try`:

```
conn.Open();
```

This opens a connection. Then you will make a SQL command, so enter the following next:

```
SqlCommand sqlComm = new SqlCommand(commandText, conn);
```

What is required for this is the text of the command. So, we'll select it from the preceding line where we wrote `Select * from dbo.People`; so, select everybody, and then you say `(command, conn)`, which is the name of the connection.

Remember that in the line that begins with `string commandText...`, the argument is the *command* and in the line below that is the *connection*. These are two different things.

Working with the SQL Server data reader

Now, in the next stage, enter the following:

```
using (SqlDataReader reader = sqlComm.ExecuteReader())
```

Here, `SqlDataReader` is a class. If you hover your mouse over it, the pop-up tooltip tells you exactly what this thing can do. Now, if you right-click on `SqlDataReader` and select and **Go to Definition**, it specifically implements this interface called `IDisposable` and all the functions that you can see if you scroll down. Further, if you right-click on `IDisposable` and select **Go to Definition**, there's `void Dispose()`, which, on expanding says, **Performs application-defined tasks associated with freeing, releasing, or resetting unmanaged resources.** This means specifically low-level disk writing and reading and so on.

Next, you see the `reader` variable in the preceding line, and `sqlComm.ExecuteReader()`, which returns an `SqlDataReader` class, as you can see in the tooltip.

Now, enter the following within a set of curly braces on the line below this:

```
while(reader.Read())
```

Now, why is this legit? Hover your mouse over `Read`, and you see that it returns a Boolean and it says, **Advances the SqlDataReader to the next record.** It returns either `true` or `false`, whether there are records left to read or not. So, enter the following within a set of curly braces below this line:

```
sampLabel.Text += $"<br>{reader[0]}, {reader[1]}, {reader[2]}";
```

 Be sure to put in the `<br>` tag, because multiple items could be returned in multiple rows, so you want to stack them vertically.

In the preceding line, 0, 1, 2 are the indices; `reader[0]`, `reader[1]`, and `reader[2]` means `column 1`, `column 2`, and `column 3`. It's the same as arrays with an index of 0.

Running the program

Now, crank up this program in your browser. Click on the **Show Records** button, and there you see the records—the Ids, the names, and the dates, as shown in *Figure 17.2.4*:

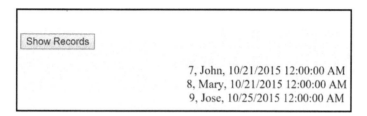

Figure 17.2.4: The results of running our program

If you right-click on this screen and select **View source**, as you can see in *Figure 17.2.5* in the highlighted region, it generates a span. Exit out of this screen and close the windows that you no longer need.

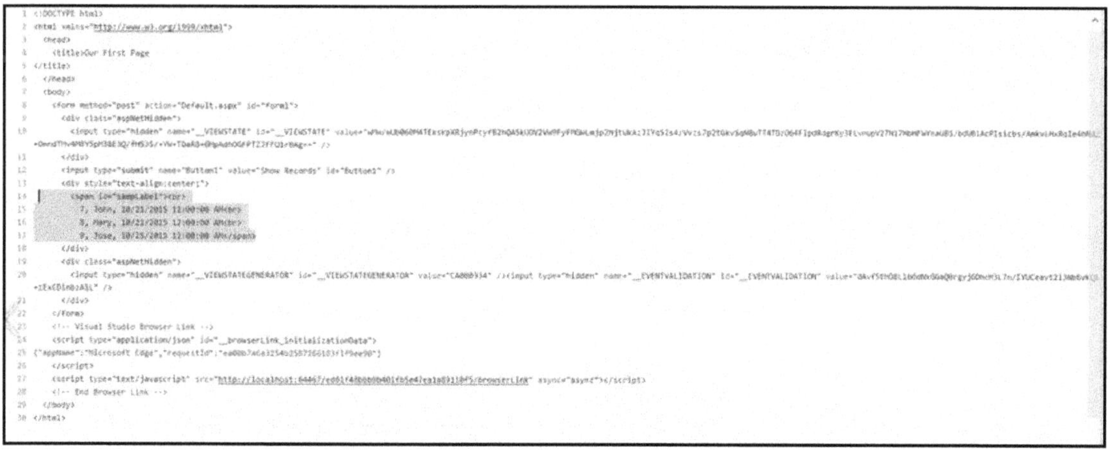

Figure 17.2.5: If you View source, you can see that it has generated a span

Chapter review

For review purposes, the complete version of the HTML file for this chapter, is shown in the following code block:

```
<!DOCTYPE html>
<html xmlns="http://www.w3.org/1999/xhtml">
  <head runat="server">
    <title>Our First Page</title>
  </head>
  <body>
    <form id="form1" runat="server">
        <asp:Button ID="Button1" runat="server" Text="Show Records"
        OnClick="Button1_Click" />
      <div style="text-align:center;">
        <asp:Label ID="sampLabel" runat="server"></asp:Label>
      </div>
    </form>
  </body>
</html>
```

The complete version of the `default.aspx.cs` file for this chapter, including comments, is shown in the following code block:

```
//using is a directive
//System is a name space
//name space is a collection of features that our needs to run
using System;
using System.Data.SqlClient;//needed for SQL commands and connections
//public means accessible anywhere
//partial means this class is split over multiple files
//class is a keyword and think of it as the outermost level of grouping
//:System.Web.UI.Page means our page inherits the features of a Page
public partial class _Default : System.Web.UI.Page
{
    protected void Button1_Click(object sender, EventArgs e)
    {
        //make connection string
        string connString = @"Data
Source=DESKTOP-4L6NSGO\SQLEXPRESS;Initial Catalog=People;Integrated
Security=True;Connect
Timeout=15;Encrypt=False;TrustServerCertificate=False;ApplicationIntent=Rea
dWrite;Mu
ltiSubnetFailover=False";
        //this is the SQL that runs against the table
        string commandText = "Select * from dbo.People";
        //using statement here helps to ensure connection is properly
```

```csharp
        //disposed of here
        using (SqlConnection conn = new SqlConnection(connString))
        {
            try
            {
                conn.Open(); //open connection
                //make command object
                SqlCommand sqlComm = new SqlCommand(commandText, conn);
                //using here helps to ensure data reader is properly
                //disposed of also
                using (SqlDataReader reader = sqlComm.ExecuteReader())
                {
                    //Read returns true while there are records to read
                    while(reader.Read())
                    {
                        //reader[0] is column 1, and so on for the
                        //other two
                        sampLabel.Text += $"<br>{reader[0]}, {reader[1]},
{reader[2]}";
                    }
                }
            }
            //a common exception occurs when the server is down and cannot
            //be reached
            catch(Exception ex)
            {
                sampLabel.Text = $"{ex.Message}";
            }
        }
    }
}
```

You can review the code and note the following, which you learned in this chapter:

1. First, the connection string, connString.
2. Then, CommandText.
3. Get SqlConnection.
4. Open it using conn.Open().
5. Make a command: SqlCommand(commandText, conn).
6. Use the SqlDataReader data reader.
7. Read the values: sampLabel.Text += $"
{reader[0]}, {reader[1]}, {reader[2]}";.
8. If there are any exceptions you can catch them using catch (Exception ex).

Summary

In this chapter, you learned how to connect to the SQL Server and then display the records from a database table in a web page. You made a connection string, connected to SQL Server, wrote the code to catch exceptions and display errors, opened the connection, and worked with the SQL Server `DataReader`.

In the next chapter, you will make a table, write a procedure, and use the procedure to insert records into the table.

18

Inserting Records into Tables Using Stored Procedures

In this chapter, you will learn how to insert records directly into a table using a *Stored procedure* that is stored in the `Programmability` folder in SQL Server. We'll do it through textboxes in the HTML page.

Adding text boxes and a button to the HTML

Crank up a project. First, let's put a couple of boxes in the **<html>** page. For this, enter the following under the line that begins with `<form id= ....`:

```
Enter Name:<asp:TextBoxID="TextBox1" runat="server"></asp:TextBox><br />
Enter Date:<asp:TextBoxID="TextBox2" runat="server"></asp:TextBox><br />
```

For the `Name` field, it is just a text box. So, for text, in other words, we'll use a string. Go to **Toolbox**, grab a `TextBox` control, and drag it in there. For the date, we will try to parse to a date time from the box.

Your `Default.aspx` screen should now look like the one shown in *Figure 18.3.1*:

```
1   <%@ Page Language="C#" AutoEventWireup="true" CodeFile="Default.aspx.cs" Inherits="_Default" %>
2
3   <!DOCTYPE html>
4
5   <html xmlns="http://www.w3.org/1999/xhtml">
6   <head runat="server">
7       <title>Our First Page</title>
8   </head>
9   <body>
10      <form id="form1" runat="server">
11      Enter Name:<asp:TextBox ID="TextBox1" runat="server"></asp:TextBox><br />
12      Enter Date:<asp:TextBox ID="TextBox2" runat="server"></asp:TextBox><br />
13          <asp:Button ID="Button1" runat="server" Text="Insert And Show" /><br />
14      <div style="text-align:center;">
15          <asp:Label ID="sampLabel" runat="server"></asp:Label>
16      </div>
17
18      </form>
19  </body>
20  </html>
21
```

Figure 18.3.1: The Default.aspx screen for this chapter

Remember, we have two boxes, we input values, and save them into the table. That's the objective here.

Next, let's also put a button in there. So again, go to **Toolbox**, grab a button, and drag and drop it just below these lines. Change the text on the button so that it's more helpful, for example, to say `Insert And Show`.

So, when you click on the button, you will insert the new records and you will also show the records to confirm that it's saved together with the existing ones.

Reviewing what you created already in SQL Server

Next, open the **SQL Server Object Explorer** screen. Now, remember that you made a database called `People` and then within it you have a table also called `People`. Further, within that you have a column called `Id`. This is the primary key. Remember, that it's auto-incremented so that you don't have to specify the ID. That is, it's done for you automatically.

Next, there are two fields: one is NAME, and the other one is DATEADDED; NAME is varchar(100) and DATEADDED is of type date. Both values have to be supplied, and that's why it says not null. The **SQL Server Object Explorer** screen up to this point is shown in *Figure 18.3.2*:

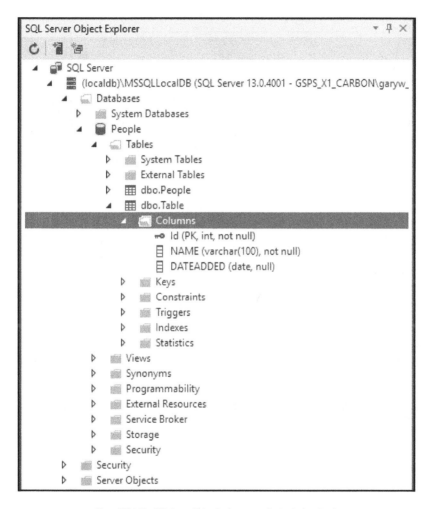

Figure 18.3.2: The SQL Server Object Explorer screen for the database People

Creating a new stored procedure

Now, expand the **Programmability** folder. There's a folder called *Stored Procedures*. Right-click on that, and select **Add New Stored Procedure...** . This is the basic stored procedure code:

```
1  ⊟CREATE PROCEDURE [dbo].[Procedure]
2        @param1 int = 0,
3        @param2 int
4   AS
5        SELECT @param1, @param2
6   RETURN 0
7
```

Figure 18.3.3: The default Stored Procedure screen

To make use of the Stored Procedure, you need to rename it first. For this, change [Procedure] in the top line to say [AddName], as follows:

```
CREATE PROCEDURE[dbo].[AddName]
```

As you can see, it's just some code that resides in SQL Server. Then you can, for example, execute that code to perform some action in the database table.

In our case, we will use this procedure to insert records into the table. We need parameters because we will enter two values. So, edit the next two lines of the Stored Procedure, as follows:

First, change param1 to Name, and change the default value of int = 0 and assign the datatype as varchar(100).

For the next line, change `param2` to `DateAdded` and it's of the `date` type. So, these are the two parameters:

```
@Name varchar(100),
@DateAdded date
```

Now, because you will not select records, rather, you will *insert* records, so, we'll enter an `insert` statement and then type the following in place of the `SELECT` line:

```
insert into People (NAME,DATEADDED) values (@Name,@DateAdded)
```

Here, you `insert into` the `People` database and then you make the list of the fields that should receive the new information, that is NAME and DATEADDED. Then, you enter `values` and then the list of parameters—`@Name` and `@DateAdded`.

Remember, the parameters in this line function similarly to the functions that you've created before. Through them, values are passed into functions when you write them in C#. The same principle applies here. Through the parameters, values are passed into the body of the stored procedure, which in this particular case, inserts to the fields, the field values directly into the table. Here, the `@Name` and `@DateAdded` values are passed into NAME and DATEADDED. That's the objective here.

The complete stored procedure is shown in *Figure 18.3.4*:

```
1  CREATE PROCEDURE [dbo].[AddName]
2      @Name varchar(100),
3      @DateAdded date
4  AS
5      insert into People (NAME,DATEADDED) values (@Name,@DateAdded)
6  RETURN 0
7
```

Figure 18.3.4: The stored procedure, dbo.AddName

Updating the database structure

Now, let's update the structure of things; so, click on the **Update** button and on **Update Database** in the dialog box that appears as shown in the *Figure 18.3.5*.

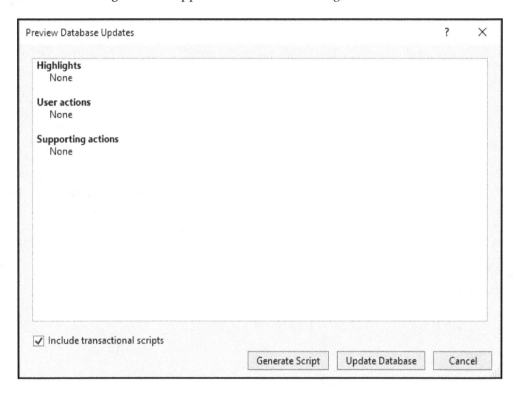

Figure 18.3.5: Preview database update dialog box

Once it's updated, expand the **Programmability** folder and then the **Stored Procedures** folder. There, you see dbo.AddName. Now, if you expand dbo.AddName, there's a list of parameters:@Name and @DateAdded.

Now, let's make use of what we've made so far. Click on the Default.aspx tab, and then go into the **Design** view, and double-click on the **Insert And Show** button. This takes us into Default.aspx.cs. Delete the Page_Load stub. We'll start with the code shown in *Figure 18.3.6* for this project:

```
1    ⊟//using is a directive
2     //System is a name space
3     //name space is a collection of features that our needs to run
4     using System;
5    ⊟//public means accessible anywhere
6     //partial means this class is split over multiple files
7     //class is a keyword and think of it as the outermost level of grouping
8     //:System.Web.UI.Page means our page inherits the features of a Page
9    ⊟public partial class _Default : System.Web.UI.Page
10    {
11   ⊟    protected void Button1_Click(object sender, EventArgs e)
12        {
13
14        }
15    }
16
```

Figure 18.3.6: The starting code for this project

Adding a namespace

Again, to make this work with SQL Server, you have to add a namespace. So, go to the top of the file, and under `using System`, enter the following:

```
using System.Data.SqlClient;//commands and connections
```

This, of course will be used for things, such as commands and connections, which you fill in as a comment. We'll do one more of these right under this line, so enter the following next:

```
using System.Data;
```

This line will also serve our purpose. There will be quite a lot of code, but it's highly sequential—it goes pretty naturally from top to bottom, and it will do the job for you.

Now, every time you click on the button, you want to clear the label so that the output doesn't continue to accumulate; so, between a set of curly braces under the line that begins with `protected void Button1_Click...`, enter the following:

```
sampLabel.Text = "";
```

Building the connection string

In the next stage, you want to get the connection string; so, on the following line you start by entering `string connString =`, followed by the @ symbol to make it a verbatim string, and then you put in the `""` symbols. Now, to get the connection string, do the following:

1. Click on **View** in the menu bar, and select **SQL Server Object Explorer**.
2. Right-click on the `People` database, and select **Properties**.
3. In the **Properties** pane, double-click on **Connection string** to select it with its long description.
4. Then, right-click on the long description and copy it.
5. Paste the description between the set of `""` symbols.

The connection string line should then look like the following:

```
string connString = @"Data Source=(localdb)\MSSQLLocalDB;Initial
Catalog=People;Integrated Security=True;Connect
Timeout=30;Encrypt=False;TrustServerCertificate=True;ApplicationIntent=Read
Write;MultiSubnetFailover=False";
```

You can now close the **SQL Server Object Explorer** and **Properties** panes.

Initializing the connection

In the next stage, because we are accessing the hard drive to read and save records, enter the following:

```
using (SqlConnection conn = new SqlConnection(connString))
```

This is how you initialize a connection. If you right-click on `SqlConnection` and select **Go to Definition**, it says that it's of the `DbConnection` type and it inherits from `SqlConnection`. Now, if you right-click on `DbConnection` and select **Go To Definition**, it says that it implements `IDisposable`. Then, if you right-click on `IDisposable` and select **Go To Definition**, it says, **Performs application-defined tasks associated with freeing, releasing, or resetting unmanaged resources.** So, for example, for low-level channels that are opened to get information from the hard drive, you've got to make sure that they are properly cleaned up. You can now close this window.

Catching exceptions

Next, because all kinds of issues can arise when you work with databases, you need to `try` it and then `catch` any exception. For this, below the open curly brace under the preceding line, enter the following:

```
try
{
}
catch (Exception ex)
```

Here, I'm really putting in `catch (Exception ex)` more for the sake of being able to display some diagnostic information. Next, between a set of curly braces below this, enter the following:

```
sampLabel.Text = $"{ex.Message}";
```

We use this line just to display the diagnostic information.

Trying out commands

Now, let's go into the `try` part. This is where everything can happen. First, let's make a command. Enter the following between the set of curly braces under `try`:

```
SqlCommand cmd = new SqlCommand();
```

Next, you'll set the type of commands, so enter the following:

```
cmd.CommandType = CommandType.StoredProcedure;
```

This line speaks for itself.

Now, to actually get the text to choose the specific stored procedure to be called, you need to enter the following next:

```
cmd.CommandText = "AddName";
```

Remember, `AddName` is what we called the procedure in the SQL Server.

Adding the parameters

Now, for the next stage, we will add what are known as *parameters*. In other words, you have to make sure that the values are actually passed into the stored procedure so that you can save them inside the table. So, enter the following next:

```
cmd.Parameters.AddWithValue("@Name", TextBox1.Text);
```

Here, we start with the name of the parameter: @Name, and then the value of it will come from the first box: TextBox1.Text.

Next, you will repeat this logic, so enter the following:

```
cmd.Parameters.AddWithValue("@DateAdded", DateTime.Parse(TextBox2.Text));
```

Here, @DateAdded is the name of the parameter, and this next stage comes from the second box: TextBox2.Text. This line will convert the value in the box, assuming that it is convertible to a DateTime object so that it matches the @DateAdded type inside the database. That is why we are taking this step.

Of course, in a more realistic situation, you might want to try DateTime.TryParse. To avoid excessive complexity, however, we'll just go with DateTime.Parse.

Enter the following next:

```
cmd.Connection = conn;
```

You have to set the conn property. We created this near the top of the file in the line that begins with using(SqlConnection conn....

For the next line, enter the following to open the connection:

```
conn.Open();
```

Saving the information for later retrieval

In the next stage, we will execute NonQuery. For this, enter the following:

```
cmd.ExecuteNonQuery();
```

This line will save the information. Now, from there forward, when you want to retrieve the information, make sure that it's working as expected. We'll just switch the type of command to CommandType of the Text type, so enter the following next:

```
cmd.CommandType = CommandType.Text;
```

Next, we will specify the text, so enter the following:

```
cmd.CommandText = "select * from dbo.People";
```

Here, `select *` means select everything from the `People` database.

After that, enter the following:

```
using (SqlDataReader reader = cmd.ExecuteReader())
```

Recognizing the role of indexers

Now, I'll show you something that I didn't show you previously. Hover your mouse over `ExecuteReader`. This returns a `SqlDataReader` class. Now, right-click on `SqlDataReader` in the preceding line and select **Go To Definition**. Do you remember when we learned about indexers earlier? Look at where it says **public override object this[string name]**. If you expand that, it says that it **Gets the value of the specified column and its native format given the column name**. If you go back, the next definition reads **public override object this[int i]**. If you expand this one, it says, **Gets the value of the specified column in its native format given the column ordinal**, here, the number of the column. So, the `public override object...` line refers to the current `SqlDataReader` object. This is basically an indexer here. Now you can see that indexers really do play a role. You can close this now.

To make use of this information, enter the following next between a set of curly braces under the previous `using` line:

```
while(reader.Read())
```

Then, between a set of curly braces below this line, enter the following:

```
sampLabel.Text += $"<br>{reader[0]}, {reader[1]}, {reader[2]}";
```

Here, after `sampLabel.Text...`, you specify `reader[0]`, `{reader[1]}`, and `{reader[2]}`, which are the three columns, accessed by the index.

You've now input the heart of the program.

Running the program

Now, let's take a look at the results. Crank this up in your browser. First, enter some values: `Berry Gibbs` for `Name`, a date, and then, click on the **Insert And Show** button. The results are shown in *Figure 18.3.7*:

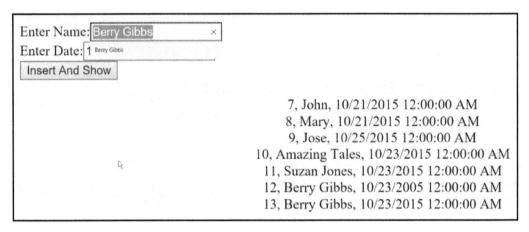

Figure 18.3.7: The initial results of running our program

So, there it is—it's working as expected. Now, let's try another one. Enter `Mark Owens` for `Name`, add a date, and then, click on the **Insert And Show** button again. As you can see in *Figure 18.3.8*, it has been added automatically. This confirms that it has been saved to the table, and then further, we can retrieve it:

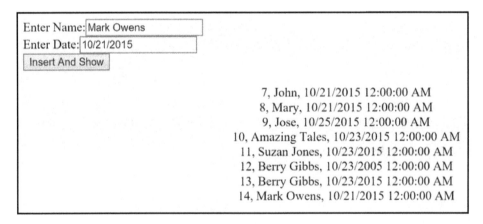

Figure 18.3.8: The modified results of running the program

So, these are the fundamentals of getting a connection.

Now consider this. Imagine, in the preceding line, I put `cmd.CommandText = "AddNames"` instead of `AddName`. In other words, I misspelled the name of the stored procedure. If I then crank this up in my browser, as seen in *Figure 18.3.9*, it says, **String was not recognized as a valid DateTime.** That's useful, right? I didn't fill `Name` or `Date`. So, it can't be converted to a `DateTime`:

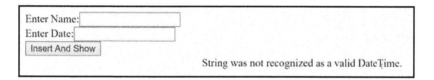

Figure 18.3.9: The results of running the program with no values entered

Now, even if I do enter values for `Name` and `Date`, it says, **Could not find stored procedure 'AddNames'**, as shown in *Figure 18.3.10*, because I misspelled the name of the stored procedure:

Enter Name: Berry Gibbs
Enter Date: 10/23/2015
Insert And Show

Could not find stored procedure 'AddNames'.

Figure 18.3.10: The results of running the program with the misspelled the name of the stored procedure

So, with the `try` line, because all of the commands after that could generate some kind of error, at least you can catch it and display the error message and you will be able to know what's going on. So, it's very useful.

Chapter review

For review, the complete version of the `Default.aspx.cs` file for this chapter, including comments, is shown in the following code block:

```
//using is a directive
//System is a name space
//name space is a collection of features that our needs to run
using System;
using System.Data.SqlClient;//commands and connections
using System.Data;
```

```
//public means accessible anywhere
//partial means this class is split over multiple files
//class is a keyword and think of it as the outermost level of grouping
//:System.Web.UI.Page means our page inherits the features of a Page
public partial class _Default : System.Web.UI.Page
{
    protected void Button1_Click(object sender, EventArgs e)
    {
        sampLabel.Text = "";
        string connString = @"Data
Source=DESKTOP-4L6NSGO\SQLEXPRESS;Initial Catalog=People;Integrated
Security=True;Connect
Timeout=15;Encrypt=False;TrustServerCertificate=False;ApplicationIntent=Rea
dWrite;MultiSubnetFailover=False";
        //put conn in a using so it can be properly closed and disposed of
        using (SqlConnection conn = new SqlConnection(connString))
        {
            try
            {
                //make sql command
                SqlCommand cmd = new SqlCommand();
                //specify type
                cmd.CommandType = CommandType.StoredProcedure;
                //write name of stored procedure inside SQL Server as
                //the name here
                cmd.CommandText = "AddName";
                //read the field box 1, and pass in through @Name
                cmd.Parameters.AddWithValue("@Name", TextBox1.Text);
                //pass in date through @DateAdded
                cmd.Parameters.AddWithValue("@DateAdded",
                DateTime.Parse(TextBox2.Text));
                //set connection property of command object
                cmd.Connection = conn;
                //open connection
                conn.Open();
                //execute the stored procedure
                cmd.ExecuteNonQuery();
                //change command type to just plain text
                cmd.CommandType = CommandType.Text;
                //write a simple SQL select statement
                cmd.CommandText = "select * from dbo.People";
                //execute reader
                using (SqlDataReader reader = cmd.ExecuteReader())
                {
                    //Read() returns true while it can read
                    while(reader.Read())
                    {
                        //reader[0] means get first column,
```

```
                    //reader uses an indexer to do this
                    sampLabel.Text += $"<br>{reader[0]}, {reader[1]},
{reader[2]}";
                }
            }
        }
        catch(Exception ex)
        {
            sampLabel.Text = $"{ex.Message}";
        }
    }
}
}
```

Summary

In this chapter, you learned how to insert records directly into a table using Stored procedures, and stored in the **Programmability** folder in the SQL Server. You created a new stored procedure, updated the database structure, built the connection string, initialized the connection, tried out commands and caught exceptions, added parameters, saved the information for later retrieval, and recognized the role of indexers.

In the next chapter, you will learn how to use the `nullable` keyword to ensure that records that have missing values can still be brought, for example, into an application.

19
Using the Nullable Feature to Make Apps More Stable

In this chapter, you will learn about using the *nullable* keyword to ensure that records that have missing values can still be brought, for example, into an application.

Adding a Show People button to the HTML

Crank up Visual Studio, and make a project. What we will do first is to put a simple button into the HTML page. For this, go to **Toolbox**, grab a `Button` control, and drop it below the line that begins with `<form id=`.... Change the text on the button to say `Show People`.

You will make a class called `Person`, and you will make that class from the database. To do this, go to the **View** menu and open **SQL Server Object Explorer**. Remember that we made a database called `People`, and it is comprised of these fields: `Id`, `NAME`, and `DATEADDED`.

Adding a field to the people database

Now, let's add one more field. Right-click on the **dbo.People** table icon, and select **View Code**. To make an additional field, type the following after `DATEADDED`:

```
SALARY decimal(18,2)
```

This is a new field type, `decimal (18,2)` means a field that is 18 units wide and has 2 decimals; that is, it's a total of 18 units wide with 2 to the right and 16 units to the left for a total of 18 units altogether. Next, click on **Update** and then the **Update Database** button in the dialog box that appears. Now, as you can see in the **SQL Server Object Explorer** pane, this field has been added, as shown in *Figure 19.4.1*:

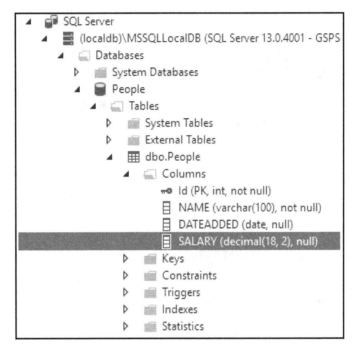

Figure 19.4.1: The Salary field has been added to dbo.People

Modifying the dbo.People table

Now, with that in place, you can modify the table. Right-click on the **dbo.People** table icon and go to **View Data**. To illustrate the concept, enter some salary amounts in a few of the rows and leave the others as NULL. Thus, a combination of databases will get NULL information. The **dbo.People** now looks like *Figure 19.4.2*:

Id	NAME	DATE...	SALA...
7	John	10/21/...	67889....
8	Mary	10/21/...	*NULL*
9	Jose	10/25/...	89877....
10	Amazi...	10/23/...	*NULL*
11	Suzan ...	10/23/...	*NULL*
12	Berry ...	10/23/...	87778...
13	Berry ...	10/23/...	34443....
14	Mark ...	10/21/...	NULL
NULL	*NULL*	*NULL*	*NULL*

dbo.People [Data] | *dbo.People.sql*

Max Rows: 1000

Figure 19.4.2: Salaries are entered into the table

If you reload it by clicking the **Refresh( )** button, it confirms that it's saved.

If you double-click on the **Salary** Column heading, it expands the column to fit.

Here, if you enter something such as 7777777777777777777 for Salary, an error message is displayed indicating **Invalid value for cell (row, column)**. So, just keep in mind that if you try to enter something like 788777.988888—it will round it automatically to two decimal places as 788777.99. So, that's basically how decimal (18,2) works: it imposes restrictions on the data that can be entered.

Writing the code for this project

In the next stage, go to the **Design** view, and double-click on the **Show People** button. This takes us into `Default.aspx.cs`. Delete the `Page_Load` block. The relevant portion of the starting code for this project should look like *Figure 19.4.3*:

```
1    //using is a directive
2    //System is a name space
3    //name space is a collection of features that our needs to run
4    using System;
5    //public means accessible anywhere
6    //partial means this class is split over multiple files
7    //class is a keyword and think of it as the outermost level of grouping
8    //:System.Web.UI.Page means our page inherits the features of a Page
9    public partial class _Default : System.Web.UI.Page
10   {
11       protected void Button1_Click(object sender, EventArgs e)
12       {
13
14       }
15   }
16
```

Figure 19.4.3: The starting code section for this project

Now, we will write code. Let's go through the creation of the code, step-by-step. First, near the top of the file under `using System,` enter the following:

```
using System.Collections.Generic;
```

We'll use this line to make a list of people. Then, also enter the following just below it:

```
using System.Data.SqlClient;
```

Creating the person class

Now for the next stage; we'll make a class called `Person`; so, enter the following just above the line that begins with `public partial class _Default...`:

```
public class Person
```

Making the properties

Next, we will make two properties. So, enter the following lines between a set of curly braces:

```
public string Name { get; set; }
public decimal? Salary { get; set; }
```

 Because the information referenced by public decimal could be missing, you put in a ? symbol. This is a *nullable* quantity, which we'll call `Salary`. This is the class.

Now, to make use of this, you have to take the following typical steps. First, you want to clear the output from the label any time somebody clicks on the button, so enter the following between a set of curly braces under the line that begins with `protected void Button1_Click...`:

```
sampLabel.Text = "";
```

Making the list of people

In the next stage, we'll make a list of people, so enter the following under this line:

```
List<Person> peopleList = new List<Person>();
```

Here, we call this as `peopleList` and set that equal to a new list of persons.

Building the connection string

In the next stage, you need to get the connection string, so, on the following line, you start by entering `string connString =`, followed by the @ symbol to make it a verbatim string, and then you put the "" symbols. Now to get the connection string, do the following:

1. Click on **View** in the menu bar and select **SQL Server Object Explorer**.
2. Right-click on the **People** database and select **Properties**.
3. In the **Properties** pane, double-click on **Connection String** to select it with its long description.
4. Then right-click on the long description and copy it.
5. Paste the description between the set of "" symbols.

The connection string line should then look like the following:

```
string connString = @"Data Source=(localdb)\MSSQLLocalDB;Initial
Catalog=People;Integrated Security=True;Connect
Timeout=30;Encrypt=False;TrustServerCertificate=True;ApplicationIntent=Read
Write;MultiSubnetFailover=False";
```

You can now close the **SQL Server Object Explorer** and **Properties** panes.

Entering the SQL-related code

Now, let's go to SQL-related code. First, enter the following below the connection string:

```
using (SqlConnection conn = new SqlConnection(connString))
```

We'll call the SQL connection, `conn`, and we will initialize the new SQL connection with the connection string.

Now, let's make a command; enter the following between a set of curly braces below this line:

```
SqlCommand comm = new SqlCommand("select * from dbo.People", conn);
```

Next, you open a connection by entering the following just below that:

```
conn.Open();
```

Next, enter the following below this line:

```
using (SqlDataReader reader = comm.ExecuteReader())
```

Adding people to the list from the table

For the next stage in the process, start by entering the following between a set of curly braces below this line:

```
while(reader.Read())
```

While this condition returns `True`, we will make objects using the information from the table in the database. In order to do that, enter the following between a set of curly braces below this line:

```
peopleList.Add(new Person() { Name = (string)reader[1], Salary = reader[3]
as decimal? });
```

Here, the first part of this line gets the column at index 1, converts it to a string, and then, assigns it to the name property of each object. Then, we say `Salary = reader[3]`, and because this is the one that could be missing a value, we say `decimal?`—as a nullable decimal, in other words.

Displaying the records

We are getting close at this point; the last stage, of course, is to display the records to see the effect of the nullable. Outside all of the curly braces beneath the `peopleList.Add...` line (as shown as follows), enter the following `foreach` statement:

```
peopleList.Add(new Person()...
    }}}foreach (Person p in peopleList)
```

Next, enter the following between a set of curly braces below this line:

```
sampLabel.Text += $"<br>{p.Name}, {p.Salary:C}";
```

This is the heart of our application.

Before running this application, once again note that an interesting piece is the `Salary` property in `...Salary = reader[3] as decimal? })`. The question mark after `as decimal` indicates that it's a nullable decimal. A decimal value could be missing, which is a different situation. If you just put `as decimal`, the tool tip would say that it's an error.

Running the program

Now, crank this up in your browser. Click on the **Show People** button. Let's examine the results, as shown in *Figure 19.4.4*:

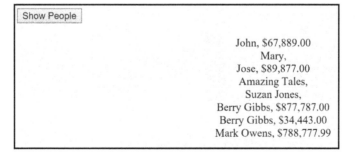

Figure 19.4.4: The results of running our program

Notice that when there's no salary, it displays just the name—it doesn't give anything else, nor does it crash. So, it's pretty good.

This is a practical application of that little symbol, the question mark, after our data type and nullable.

Chapter review

For review, the complete version of the `Default.aspx.cs` file for this chapter, including comments, is shown in the following code block:

```
//using is a directive
//System is a name space
//name space is a collection of features that our needs to run
using System;
using System.Collections.Generic; //needed for lists
using System.Data.SqlClient;//needed for commands and connections
//public means accessible anywhere
//partial means this class is split over multiple files
//class is a keyword and think of it as the outermost level of grouping
//:System.Web.UI.Page means our page inherits the features of a Page
public class Person
{
    public string Name { get; set; }
    public decimal? Salary { get; set;}
}
public partial class _Default : System.Web.UI.Page
{
    protected void Button1_Click(object sender, EventArgs e)
    {
        //clear label text every button click
        sampLabel.Text = "";
        //make list of people
        List<Person> peopleList = new List<Person>();
        //get connection string form SQL Server
        string connString = @"Data
Source=DESKTOP-4L6NSGO\SQLEXPRESS;Initial
        Catalog=People;Integrated Security=True;Connect
Timeout=15;Encrypt=False;TrustServerCertificate=False;ApplicationIntent=Rea
dWrite;MultiSubnetFailover=False";
        //make connection, be sure it's in a using so it's properly
        //disposed of
        using (SqlConnection conn = new SqlConnection(connString))
        {
            //make sql command
```

```
            SqlCommand comm = new SqlCommand("select * from dbo.People",
conn);

            //open connection
            conn.Open();
            //make reader, be sure it's inside a using so it's properly
            //disposed of
            using (SqlDataReader reader = comm.ExecuteReader())
            {
                while (reader.Read())
                {
                    //add new people to list, noting that reader[3]
                    //could be null, so do it as "as decimal?"
                    //nullable decimal
                    peopleList.Add(new Person() { Name = (string)reader[1],
                    Salary = reader[3] as decimal? });
                }
            }
        }
        //display list of people, formatting salary as currency
        foreach(Person p in peopleList)
        {
            sampLabel.Text += $"<br>{p.Name}, {p.Salary:C}";
        }
    }
}
```

Summary

In this chapter, you learned about using the *nullable* keyword to ensure that records that have missing values can still be brought, for example, into an application. You added a field to the `People` database, modified the `dbo.people` table, created a `Person` class, made a list of people, built a connection string, entered SQL-related code, and added people to the list from the `dbo.people` table.

In the next chapter, you will learn about dragging charts into the page and then making them work with some simple tables inside the SQL Server through C# as the language that connects the page and the database.

20

Connecting a Chart Control to SQL Server

In this chapter, you will learn about how to drag charts into the page and then make them work with some simple tables inside SQL Server through C# as the language that connects the page and the database.

Placing a chart into the HTML page

Crank up a project and what we will do first is to place a chart in the **<html>** page. Go to **Toolbox** (*Ctrl* + *Alt* + *X*), enter char... in the **Search** field, and drag and drop it below the line that begins with <form id=....

As you can see on your screen, this generates all of the following markup. You can leave it as is. It's sufficient for our purposes:

```
<asp:Chart ID="Chart1"runat="server">
  <Series>
    <asp:SeriesName="Series1" ChartType="Point"></asp:Series>
  </Series>
  <ChartAreas>
    <asp:ChartArea Name="ChartArea1"></asp:ChartArea>
  </ChartAreas>
</asp:Chart>
```

You can delete the two <div... lines and the <asp:Label ID... line. We don't need them.

Adding a button to the HTML page

Next, you need to place a button below the `</asp:Chart>` line. So again, go to **Toolbox**, grab a `Button` control, and drag it in there. Change the text on the button to say **Load Data**. Here, `Load Data` means loading and displaying it in the chart.

Notice that, when you drag in a chart, the page adds the entire block shown as follows, at the top of `System.Web.UI.DataVisualization.Charting`:

```
<%@Register Assembly="System.Web.DataVisualization, Version=4.0.0.0,
Culture=neutral, PublicKeyToken=31bf3856ad364e35"
Namespace="System.Web.UI.DataVisualization.Charting" TagPrefix="asp" %>
```

Adding a new table to the People database

Now, for the next stage, click on **View** in the menu bar, and select **SQL Server Object Explorer**. You have to add a new table, so in the `People` database, right-click on the **Tables** folder and select **Add New Table...** . Your screen should look like the one shown in *Figure 20.5.1:*

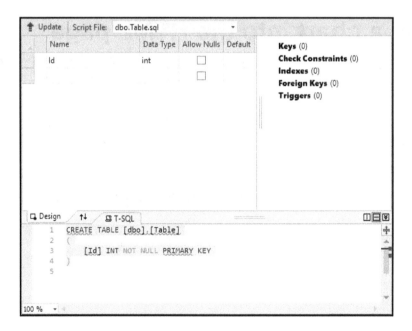

Figure 20.5.1: A blank new table

Next, type XValues in the Id field, and then click in the **Data Type field**. Start to type decimal, and notice that decimal(18,0) shows up automatically. Now change this to (18,3). This simply means a field that is 18 wide and has 3 decimal places; that is, it's a total of 18 wide with 3 to the right and 15 to the left for a total of 18 altogether. The **Allow Nulls** box should be checked for this field. It's the same thing for YValues. Imagine that we've done an experiment, and we've measured some quantities. So, enter YValues in the Id field, decimal(18,3) in the data type field, and leave the **Allow Nulls** box checked for this field.

Next, right-click on **Id** and select **Set Primary Key**.

Enabling auto-incrementation

Next, you want to enable auto-incrementation, so specifically that means the following:

1. First, rename the table to ExperimentValues, as follows:

```
CREATE TABLE [dbo].[ExperimentValues]
```

2. After PRIMARY KEY, put identity(1,1), as follows:

```
[Id] INT NOT NULL PRIMARY KEY identity(1,1),
```

Here, identity(1,1), as you learned previously, means that this field will grow by 1, beginning from 1, every time you add a new record. So, this is the structure of our table, as shown in *Figure 20.5.2*:

```
1  CREATE TABLE [dbo].[ExperimentValues]
2  (
3      [Id] INT NOT NULL PRIMARY KEY identity (1,1),
4      [XValues] DECIMAL(18, 3) NULL,
5      [YValues] DECIMAL(18, 3) NULL,
6  )
7
```

Figure 20.5.2: The structure of our table for this chapter

Adding values to the new table

Next, click on the **Update** button. Click on **Update Database** in the dialog box that appears.

Now, you have `ExperimentValues`. Right-click on it, select **View Data**, and let's add some values, as shown in *Figure 20.5.3*:

Id	XValues	YValues
1	5000.000	10000.000
2	30.000	45.000
3	3.450	99.000
4	23.000	45.000
▶* NULL	NULL	NULL

Figure 20.5.3: Values added to the ExperimentValues table

Now, we've got some values in a table. Notice again that the **Id** field is auto incremented—it begins at **1** and grows by 1 every time you add a new record. Close the table windows and go back into `Default.aspx.cs`.

Now, double-click on the **Design** button, and a little chart appears, as shown in *Figure 20.5.4*:

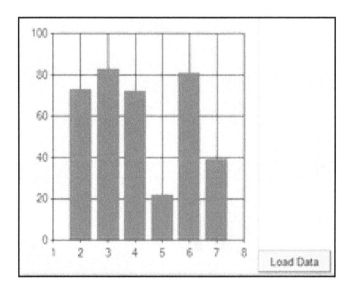

Figure 20.5.4: Theoretical preview of the data in the ExperimentValues table

Coding the project

This chart does not represent the real data yet. It is just a theoretical preview. So, double-click on the **Load Data** button, which brings up the event handler in `Default.aspx.cs`. Delete the `Page_Load` stub. We'll start with the code shown in *Figure 20.5.5* for this project:

```
1     //using is a directive
2     //System is a name space
3     //name space is a collection of features that our needs to run
4     using System;
5     //public means accessible anywhere
6     //partial means this class is split over multiple files
7     //class is a keyword and think of it as the outermost level of grouping
8     //:System.Web.UI.Page means our page inherits the features of a Page
9     public partial class _Default : System.Web.UI.Page
10    {
11
12        protected void Button1_Click(object sender, EventArgs e)
13        {
14    |
15        }
16    }
17
```

Figure 20.5.5: The starting code for this project

Adding a namespace

The first thing is you have to add a namespace. So, go to the top of the file, and under `using System`, enter the following:

```
using System.Data.SqlClient;
```

This line is used for connections and commands.

Building the connection string

In the next stage, you need the connection string. So, on the following line you start by entering `string connString =`, followed by the @ symbol to make it a verbatim string, and then you put the `""` symbols. Now, to get the connection string, do the following:

1. Click on **View** in the menu bar, and select **SQL Server Object Explorer**.
2. Right-click on the **People** database, and select **Properties**.
3. In the **Properties** pane, double-click on **Connection String** to select it with its long description.
4. Then, right-click on the long description and copy it.
5. Paste the description between the set of `""` symbols.

The connection string line should then look like the following:

```
string connString = @"Data Source=(localdb)\MSSQLLocalDB;Initial
Catalog=People;Integrated Security=True;Connect
Timeout=30;Encrypt=False;TrustServerCertificate=True;ApplicationIntent=Read
Write;MultiSubnetFailover=False";
```

This is the connection string specific to your computer. You can now close the **SQL Server Object Explorer** and **Properties** panes.

Now, enter the following beneath this line:

```
using (SqlConnection conn = new SqlConnection(connString))
```

Writing a SQL query

Next, you'll make the `commandText` variable. So, between a set of curly braces, enter the following:

```
string commandText = "select XValues, YValues from dbo.ExperimentValues";
```

To define the text, you have to write the actual SQL query, so you type `select XValues, YValues from dbo.ExperimentValues`. This will select `XValues` and `YValues` from those two column names in the `ExperimentValues` table.

Making the command object

Now, you need to make the command object, so enter the following next:

```
SqlCommand command = new SqlCommand(commandText, conn);
```

Here you pass in the two relevant quantities, the two arguments, so specifically, `(commandText, conn)`.

Opening the connection and making a SQL data reader

In the next stage, you will open a connection, so enter the following below the preceding line:

```
conn.Open();
```

Then you'll make a SQL data reader, so enter the following next:

```
SqlDataReader reader = command.ExecuteReader();
```

This line will get the data that we need.

Now that you've done all of that, type the following below the preceding line:

```
Chart1.DataBindTable(reader, "XValues");
```

Note that we include the name of the column, `XValues`, which is to serve as the labeling for the *x*-axis. So, the *x*-axis is the horizontal axis.

Running the program

This is the heart of the application. Crank it up in your browser, and click on the **Load Data** button.

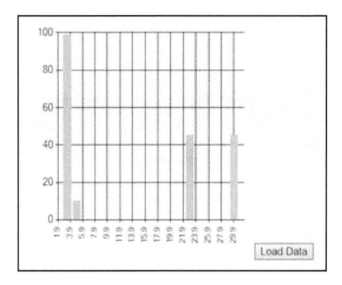

Figure 20.5.6: Display of The actual data from the ExperimentValues table

Here's the data, as shown in *Figure 20.5.6*. It has the values along the horizontal and vertical axes.

Modifying the program to display the Y values

If you wanted to, just to show you how easy it is, you could change the following line to the Y values. In other words, you can flip them around:

```
Chart1.DataBindTable(reader, "YValues");
```

Now, crank it up in your browser, and click on the **Load Data** button once again. The results are shown in *Figure 20.5.7*:

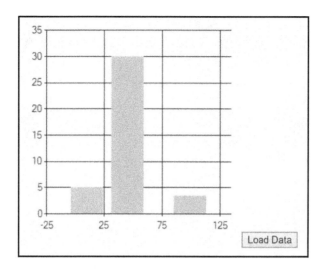

Figure 20.5.7: Chart of the Values from the ExperimentValues table

Now you see that it looks very different. So that's how you can make simple charts. Now save this. This is the whole application.

Chapter review

Let's review what we did: you built the connection string and finished making the connection inside the `using (SqlConnection conn...` line so that the connection could be properly disposed of. Then, you wrote the query string, made the command object, opened a connection, and executed the reader. Finally, you used `DataBind` to bind the database table to the charts so that you could display the results.

The complete version of the `Default.aspx.cs` file for this chapter, including comments, is shown in the following code block:

```
//using is a directive
//System is a name space
//name space is a collection of features that our needs to run
using System;
using System.Data.SqlClient;
//public means accessible anywhere
//partial means this class is split over multiple files
//class is a keyword and think of it as the outermost level of grouping
//:System.Web.UI.Page means our page inherits the features of a Page
public partial class _Default : System.Web.UI.Page
{
```

```
    protected void Button1_Click(object sender, EventArgs e)
    {
        //make connection string
        string connString = @"Data
Source=DESKTOP-4L6NSGO\SQLEXPRESS;Initial Catalog=People;Integrated
Security=True;Connect
Timeout=15;Encrypt=False;TrustServerCertificate=False;ApplicationIntent=Rea
dWrite;MultiSubnetFailover=False";
        //enclose connection making inside a using so connection is
        //properly disposed of
        using (SqlConnection conn = new SqlConnection(connString))
        {
            //make command text
            string commandText = "select XValues, YValues from
dbo.ExperimentValues";
            //make command object
            SqlCommand command = new SqlCommand(commandText, conn);
            //open connection
            conn.Open();
            //execute reader to read values from table
            SqlDataReader reader = command.ExecuteReader();
            //bind chart to table do display the results
            Chart1.DataBindTable(reader, "XValues");
        }
    }
}
```

Summary

In this chapter, you learned about dragging charts into the page and then making them work with some simple tables inside SQL Server through C# as the language that connects the page and the database. You placed a chart into the HTML page, added a new table to the People database, enabled auto-incrementation, added values to the new table, added a namespace, built a connection string, wrote a SQL query, opened the connection and made a SQL data reader, ran the program, and finally modified it to display the Y values.

In the next chapter, you will learn how to use LINQ together with SQL and SQL Server.

21

Using LINQ to Operate on Tables from SQL Server

In this chapter, you will learn how to use LINQ together with SQL and SQL Server.

Changing the data in the ExperimentValues table

We will be working with the database table that we created in the previous chapter called ExperimentValues, as shown in *Figure 21.6.1*:

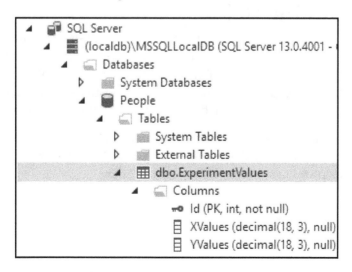

Figure 21.6.1: The ExperimentValues table from chapter 20

Remember that the table has an Id field (**PK, primary key integer**, and **not null**) and then XValues (decimal, (18, 3), which means 18 units wide with 3 decimal places and then 15 units to the left for 18 units altogether. You can make this null if you want. Likewise, with YValues, (decimal, (18, 3); so, 3 places to the right of the decimal, and 15 units to the left for 18 units altogether.

Now make sure that you have data in there. So, right-click on dbo.ExperimentValues and select **View Data**. You should see the data that we entered in the previous chapter. Of course, you can always change it. To make things easier, let's change the values to those shown in *Figure 21.6.2*:

Id	XValues	YValues
1	1000.000	5000.000
2	2000.000	10000.000
3	3000.000	15000.000
4	4000.000	20000.000
NULL	NULL	NULL

Figure 21.6.2: The new data for the ExperimentValues table

If you want, you can reload it to see that it's saved. So that's our simple database table.

Summarizing the fields

Now we will reach into it and summarize the fields. You will find the sum of the X values and the sum of the Y values using LINQ. First, go into **<html>** and place a button below the line that begins with <form id= . . . . . Go to **Toolbox** (*Ctrl + Alt + X*), grab a Button control, and drag it in there. Change the text on the button to say **Sum Fields**. Of course, several other operations can be performed. This is just one operation: summation.

Close **Toolbox** and switch to the **Design** view. Double-click on the **Sum Fields** button. This takes us into Default.aspx.cs. Delete the Page_Load block. The relevant portion of the starting code for this project should look like *Figure 21.6.3*:

```
1    //using is a directive
2    //System is a name space
3    //name space is a collection of features that our needs to run
4    using System;
5    //public means accessible anywhere
6    //partial means this class is split over multiple files
7    //class is a keyword and think of it as the outermost level of grouping
8    //:System.Web.UI.Page means our page inherits the features of a Page
9    public partial class _Default : System.Web.UI.Page
10   {
11
12       protected void Button1_Click(object sender, EventArgs e)
13       {
14
15       }
16   }
17
```

Figure 21.6.3: The starting code section for this project

Adding the namespaces

First, near the top of the file under `using System`, enter the following lines, all of which are necessary:

```
using System.Data.SqlClient;
using System.Linq;
using System.Data;
```

Building the connection string

The next stage will be to make a connection string, so within a set of curly braces below the line that begins with `protected void Button1_Click...`, start by entering `string connString =`, followed by the @ symbol to make it a verbatim string, and then you put the `""` symbols. Now to get the connection string, do the following:

1. Click on **View** in the menu bar, and select **SQL Server Object Explorer**.
2. Right-click on the `People` database, and select **Properties**.
3. In the **Properties** pane, double-click on **Connection String** to select it with its long description.

4. Then right-click on the long description and copy it.
5. Paste the description between a set of " " symbols.

The connection string line should then look like the following:

```
string connString = @"Data Source=(localdb)\MSSQLLocalDB;Initial
Catalog=People;Integrated Security=True;Connect
Timeout=30;Encrypt=False;TrustServerCertificate=True;ApplicationIntent=Read
Write;MultiSubnetFailover=False";
```

You can now close the **SQL Server Object Explorer** and **Properties** panes.

Making the SQL connection

In the next stage, we will proceed as usual. So, enter the following line:

```
using (SqlConnection conn = new SqlConnection(connString))
```

Notice, as you type this, you see that `SqlClient` in the `using System.Data.SqlClient;` line at the top of the file becomes active. It changes to black. This means that the SQL connection is stored there, and if you hover your mouse over it, it also tells you that this is the case: **class System.Data.SqlClient.SqlConnection**

In the next stage, enter the following between a set of curly braces below this line:

```
SqlCommand command = new SqlCommand("select * from dbo.ExperimentValues",
conn);
```

Between the parentheses that follow `SqlCommand()`, you put the text that defines the command directly into the constructor as an argument. Remember, you already have `ExperimentValues`. The * symbol means select all of the columns. So, you need the command text and then the connection.

Making an adapter

Next, you will make an adapter. So, enter the following:

```
SqlDataAdapter adapter = new SqlDataAdapter(command);
```

Here, `SqlDataAdapter` is something that exists between the actual database and us. It's a way of adapting the information from here to there, so to speak. To initialize it, you can pass in a specific SQL command. So, in our case we will pass in `(command)`. You can add the comment, `//make adapter`, following this line.

Making a data table

Next, you'll make a data table, as follows:

```
DataTable dt = new DataTable();
```

Again, notice that, once you type `DataTable`, the `using System.Data;` namespace at the top of the file becomes active. So, if hover your mouse over `DataTable`, it says **class System.Data.DataTable**. This is where it's stored. So, it's stored at the `Data` namespace.

Populating the table with data

Now we need to fill this table with some information. So, enter the following next:

```
adapter.Fill(dt);
```

Here, you type the name of the adapter, and then the dataset to be filled. So, with these three lines, first you make an adapter and get information using a SQL command, and then you make a data table. Then you use the adapter to fill that table. Now we can make use of it as follows:

```
var summedXValues = dt.AsEnumerable().Sum(row => row.Field<decimal>(1));
```

Here, we can take that data table and make it enumerable so that we can go through it. Note that we're throwing a Lambda expression in there using =>; `<decimal>` is the data type, and then, if you hover your mouse over the parentheses after `<decimal>()`, the tooltip says (`DataColumn column`): **Provides strongly-typed access to each of the columns values in the specified row.** So, insert a 1 between the parentheses.

Next, enter the following for the `summedYValues` variable, and note that we put a 2 between the parentheses:

```
var summedYValues = dt.AsEnumerable().Sum(row => row.Field<decimal>(2));
```

Once you have entered all of that, then you can display the sum of the x and y values, so enter the following lines next:

```
sampLabel.Text = $"Sum of y values={summedYValues}";
sampLabel.Text += $"<br>Sum of x values={summedXValues}";
```

Displaying the summed values

In the preceding lines, note that the first line does not need a `<br>` tag, but the next line does. Also, the first line just needs =, while the next line needs += to append.

Running the program

Remember, the idea is to sum the fields, so open your browser and click on the **Sum Fields** button:

Sum Fields

Sum of y values=50.000
Sum of x values=10.000

Figure 21.6.4: The initial results of running our program

You can see that the **Sum of Y values** is **50.000**, and the **Sum of X values** is **10.000**. You can confirm that this is working as expected by opening the **SQL Server Object Explorer** pane, right-clicking on the `ExperimentValues` table, and adding up the values, as seen in *Figure 21.6.5*:

Id	XValues	YValues
1	1.000	5.000
2	2.000	10.000
3	3.000	15.000
4	4.000	20.000
NULL	NULL	NULL

Figure 21.6.5: Add the values in the X and Y columns

The **XValues** column adds up to 10.000, and the **YValues** column adds up to 50.000. Both of these sums check with the results of the program run.

Close the `ExperimentValues` table window and the **SQL Object Explorer** pane. This is working as expected again.

Adding comments

Now add this comment above the connection string line:

```
//make connection string
```

Whenever you deal with low-level resources, apply a `using` block. Add the following comment above the line that begins with `using (SqlConnection conn...`:

```
//make connection object
```

Remember, the purpose is to make it, use it, and dispose off it properly so that there are no memory leaks remaining. Do that whenever you're dealing with hard drive access, for example.

Add the following comment above the line that begins with `SqlCommand command =...`:

```
//make SQL command
```

Then, add the following comment above the line that begins with `sqlDataAdapter adapter...` to emphasize the purpose of the adapter:

```
//make adapter object and pass in the command
```

Also, add this comment at the very end of the line:

```
//make adapter
```

Next, for `DataTable dt...`, add this comment:

```
//make table
```

The adapter is the mechanism that allows us to fill the table, so add the following comment at the end of the `adapter.Fill(dt);` line:

```
//fill table with adapter
```

Next, add the following comment above line 30:

```
//lines 30 - 31 use LINQ to sum each column
```

Finally, add the following comment above line 33:

```
//lines 33-34 display the results in the web page
```

In the following line, notice that the field here is `decimal`, because that's how we made it in SQL Server, and 1 simply means the first field and the index is 1. However, recall that this really means the second column because there are three columns:

```
var summedXValues = dt.AsEnumerable().Sum(row => row.Field<decimal>(1));
```

As can be seen in *Figure 21.6.6*, **Id** is really index 0, **XValues** is index 1, and **YValues** is index 2. This is why we use 1 and 2 here, because there are three columns where the second column is at index 1:

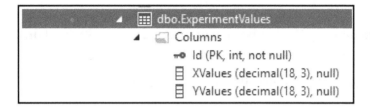

Figure 21.6.6: Id is index 0, XValues is index 1, and YValues is index 2

Chapter review

The complete version of the `Default.aspx.cs` file for this chapter, including comments, is shown in the following code block.

```
//using is a directive
//System is a name space
//name space is a collection of features that our needs to run
using System;
using System.Data.SqlClient;
using System.Linq;
using System.Data;
//public means accessible anywhere
//partial means this class is split over multiple files
//class is a keyword and think of it as the outermost level of grouping
//:System.Web.UI.Page means our page inherits the features of a Page
public partial class _Default : System.Web.UI.Page
{
    protected void Button1_Click(object sender, EventArgs e)
    {
        //make connection string
        string connString = @"Data
Source=DESKTOP-4L6NSGO\SQLEXPRESS;Initial Catalog=People;Integrated
Security=True;Connect
Timeout=15;Encrypt=False;TrustServerCertificate=False;ApplicationIntent=Rea
```

```
dWrite;MultiSubnetFailover=False";
        //make connection object
        using (SqlConnection conn = new SqlConnection(connString))
        {
            //make sql command
            SqlCommand command = new SqlCommand("select * from
dbo.ExperimentValues", conn);
            //make adapter object and pass in the command
            //make adapter
            SqlDataAdapter adapter = new SqlDataAdapter(command);
            //make table
            DataTable dt = new DataTable();
            adapter.Fill(dt); //fill table with adapter
            //lines 30 - 31 use linq to sum each column
            var summedXValues = dt.AsEnumerable().Sum(row => row.Field<
            decimal>(1));
            var summedYValues = dt.AsEnumerable().Sum(row => row.Field<
            decimal>(2));
            //lines 33-34 display the results in the web page
            sampLabel.Text = $"Sum of y values={summedYValues}";
            sampLabel.Text += $"<br>Sum of x values={summedXValues}";
        }
    }
}
```

Summary

In this chapter, you learned how to use LINQ together with SQL and SQL Server. You changed the data in the ExperimentValues table, wrote code to summarize the fields using LINQ, added namespaces, built the connection string, made the SQL connection, made the adapter, made the data table, populated the table with data, displayed the summed values, ran the program, and finally added comments.

In the next chapter, you will learn how to make a page, save stuff from the page to a hard drive, and then read it back.

22

Creating a Page That Saves Text to Disk

In this chapter, you will learn how you can make a page, save stuff from the page to a hard drive, and then read it back.

Creating an application to save text

By the end of this chapter, you'll have made a little application like the one shown in *Figure 22.1.1*. For **Save Location**, you can enter something like c:\data\samp.txt, to save a text file:

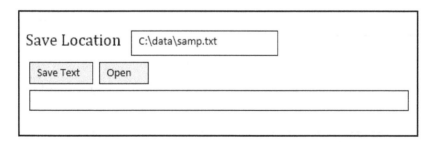

Figure 22.1.1: A user interface similar to the one you will build for the application in this chapter

Then, you can enter some text, such as This is some sample text to be saved.:

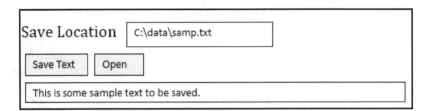

Figure 22.1.2: The Save Location with some sample text entered in the application

Now click on the **Save Text** button. This brings up Notepad to confirm that it's been saved, as shown in *Figure 22.1.3*:

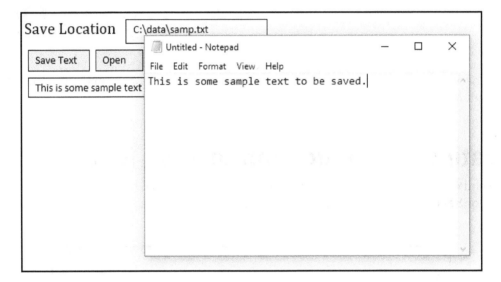

Figure 22.1.3: The sample text is saved, and it brings up Notepad

If you want, you can also open the text back in the page. So, click **Open** and then it's saved in the page, as shown in *Figure 22.1.4*:

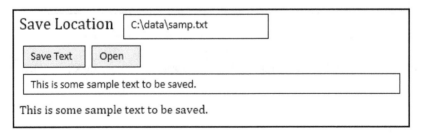

Figure 22.1.4: The sample text is saved in the page

Further, if you didn't specify your path, obviously that will result in an error, as shown in *Figure 22.1.5*. In this case, it displays the **Empty path name is not legal.** message:

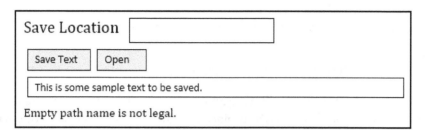

Figure 22.1.5: Error message displayed when no Save Location is entered

So, that's the objective here. Keep this example in mind.

Now let's create a project. Go to **File** | **New** | **Web Site...** Then, from the **View** menu, go to **Solution Explorer**, and click on **Default.aspx**.

Creating the user interface for your project

First, you have to build your user interface, so you will need a text box in the HTML page, where you can input the path. For this, go to **Toolbox**, grab a `TextBox` control, and drop it below the line that begins with `<form id=`.... Enter the words `Save Path` at the beginning of this line, as follows:

```
Save Path:<asp:TextBoxID="TextBox1"runat="server"></asp:TextBox><br/>
```

Next, you'll have a button that basically acts to open the saved file in the web page, so change the text in the button to say to `Open In Page`, as follows:

```
<asp:Button ID="Button1"runat="server"Text="Open In Page" /><br />
```

In this context, it just means reading the simple text back into the page. Now go into the **Design** view to see the user interface thus far, as shown in *Figure 22.1.6*:

Figure 22.1.6: The user interface thus far

Next, you also need a place to enter the text to be saved. So, grab another `TextBox` control, and enter `Text To Be Saved` at the beginning of this line, as follows:

```
Text To Be
Saved:<asp:TextBoxID="TextBox2"runat="server"Width="1069px"></asp:TextBox><
br/>
```

Delete the two `<div>` lines—you won't need them.

Now let's add a `Save` button. So, we'll have an **Open in Page** button and a **Save** button. Now, drag in a button from **Toolbox**, and place it above `Button1`. (The layout is up to you, of course.) Change the text as follows:

```
<asp:Button ID="Button2"runat="server"Text="Save" /><br />
```

The complete HTML file for this project is shown in the following code block.

```
<%@ Page Language="C#" AutoEventWireup="true" CodeFile="Default.aspx.cs"
Inherits="_Default" %>
<!DOCTYPE html>
<html xmlns="http://www.w3.org/1999/xhtml">
  <head runat="server">
    <title>Our First Page</title>
  </head>
  <body>
    <form id="form1" runat="server">
      Save Path:<asp:TextBox ID="TextBox1" runat="server"></asp:TextBox>
      <br />
      <asp:Button ID="Button2" runat="server" Text="Save"
      OnClick="Button2_Click" />
      <br />
      <asp:Button ID="Button1" runat="server" Text="Open In Page"
      OnClick="Button1_Click" />
      <br />
      Text To Be Saved:<asp:TextBox ID="TextBox2" runat="server"
      Width="1069px"></asp:TextBox>
      <br />
      <asp:Label ID="sampLabel" runat="server"></asp:Label>
    </form>
  </body>
</html>
```

Now, if you go into the **Design** view, a simple interface is displayed, as shown in *Figure 22.1.7*:

```
|body|
Save Path:
Save
    Open In Page
Text to be saved:
                                                              [sampLabel]
```

Figure 22.1.7: The complete simple user interface

If you like, you can drag on a corner of the Text To Be Saved box and enlarge it so that you have a bigger place to save your text. So now you have a place to save, a **Save** button, **Open In page**, and sampLabel. That's sufficient for our purposes.

Starting to code the project

Now, double-click on the **Save** button. This takes us into Default.aspx.cs. Delete the Page_Load block. The relevant portion of the starting code for this project should look like *Figure 22.1.8*:

```
1    //using is a directive
2    //System is a name space
3    //name space is a collection of features that our needs to run
4    using System;
5                            //public means accessible anywhere
6                            //partial means this class is split over multiple files
7                            //class is a keyword and think of it as the outermost level of grouping
8                            //:System.Web.UI.Page means our page inherits the features of a Page
9    public partial class _Default : System.Web.UI.Page
10   {
11       protected void Button2_Click(object sender, EventArgs e)
12       {
13
14       }
15   }
16
```

Figure 22.1.8: The starting code for this project

So, for the **Save** button code, you have to add a namespace. First, near the top of the file under using System, enter the following:

```
using System.IO;
```

Catching an exception

Let's make use of this. Now, because it's possible that someone didn't enter something in the box, an error message could be generated and you want to catch it. So, beneath the open curly brace under the line that begins with `protected void Button2_Click...`, enter the following:

```
try
{

}
catch(Exception ex)
{
    sampLabel.Text = ex.Message;
}
```

The preceding `sampLabel.Text` line is used to display the message from the exception that is generated and caught.

Creating a StreamWriter class

Next, we will use a `StreamWriter` class. This class gets low-level access to hard drives, and so on, so you've got to make sure that it's within a `using` statement. You need to be able to create it, use it, and dispose off it completely. So, enter the following between a set of curly braces below `try`:

```
using (StreamWriter sw = new StreamWriter(TextBox1.Text))
```

To initialize this class, the argument to be passed in is `TextBox1.Text`. So this is the one that will write to the file. To confirm, you can go to the **Source** view in `Default.aspx`, and verify that `Save Path` is TextBox1.

Now, to actually write to the file, enter the following between a set of curly braces under the previous statement:

```
sw.Write(TextBox2.Text);
```

Here, `sw` is a stream writer, `sw.write` is a method that it has, a function, and then you'll take that `TextBox2` stuff and write it. So, from `TextBox1`, you get the path, and from `TextBox2`, you take the text out.

Now, if you right-click on `StreamWriter` and select **Go To Definition**, the result looks like the screen shown in *Figure 22.1.9*:

```
1   ⊞Assembly mscorlib, Version=4.0.0.0, Culture=neutral, PublicKeyToken=b77a5c561934e089
4
5   ⊞using [...]
9
10  ⊟namespace System.IO
11   {
12  ⊞    [...]public class StreamWriter : TextWriter
15        {
16  ⊞        [...]public static readonly StreamWriter Null;
18
19  ⊞        [...]public StreamWriter(Stream stream);
21            public StreamWriter(string path);
22  ⊞        [...]public StreamWriter(Stream stream, Encoding encoding);
24            public StreamWriter(string path, bool append);
25  ⊞        [...]public StreamWriter(Stream stream, Encoding encoding, int bufferSize);
27            public StreamWriter(string path, bool append, Encoding encoding);
28  ⊞        [...]public StreamWriter(Stream stream, Encoding encoding, int bufferSize, bool leaveOpen);
30  ⊞        [...]public StreamWriter(string path, bool append, Encoding encoding, int bufferSize);
32
33  ⊞        [...]public virtual bool AutoFlush { get; set; }
35  ⊞        [...]public virtual Stream BaseStream { get; }
37  ⊞        [...]public override Encoding Encoding { get; }
39
40            public override void Close();
41  ⊞        [...]public override void Flush();
43  ⊞        [...]public override Task FlushAsync();
46  ⊞        [...]public override void Write(char value);
48  ⊞|       [...]public override void Write(char[] buffer, int index, int count);
50  ⊞        [...]public override void Write(string value);
52  ⊞        [...]public override void Write(char[] buffer);
54  ⊞        [...]public override Task WriteAsync(char value);
57  ⊞        [...]public override Task WriteAsync(string value);
60  ⊞        [...]public override Task WriteAsync(char[] buffer, int index, int count);
63  ⊞        [...]public override Task WriteLineAsync();
66  ⊞        [...]public override Task WriteLineAsync(char value);
69  ⊞        [...]public override Task WriteLineAsync(string value);
72  ⊞        [...]public override Task WriteLineAsync(char[] buffer, int index, int count);
75  ⊞        [...]protected override void Dispose(bool disposing);
77        }
78   }
```

Figure 22.1.9: The definition of StreamWriter

At the very bottom, you can see that it's got `Dispose`, and you can see near the top that `StreamWriter` inherits from `TextWriter`. Next, if you select **Go To Definition** of `TextWriter`, you can see that there's `IDisposable`, as shown in *Figure 22.1.10*:

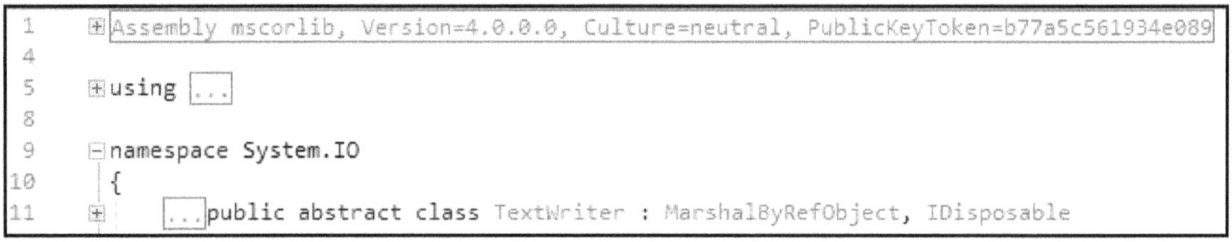

```
1      ⊞Assembly mscorlib, Version=4.0.0.0, Culture=neutral, PublicKeyToken=b77a5c561934e089
4
5      ⊞using ...
8
9      ⊟namespace System.IO
10     {
11     ⊞     ...public abstract class TextWriter : MarshalByRefObject, IDisposable
```

Figure 22.1.10: The definition of TextWriter

If you right click on `IDisposable` and select **Go To Definition**, there's `Dispose`, as shown in *Figure 22.1.11*:

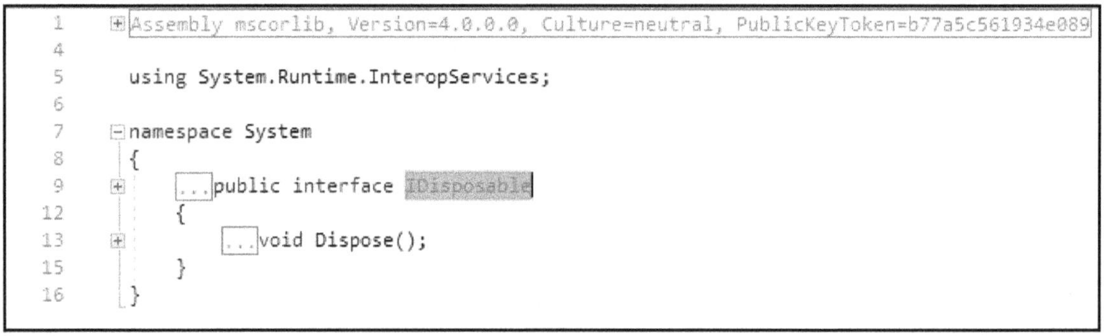

```
1      ⊞Assembly mscorlib, Version=4.0.0.0, Culture=neutral, PublicKeyToken=b77a5c561934e089
4
5      using System.Runtime.InteropServices;
6
7      ⊟namespace System
8      {
9      ⊞     ...public interface IDisposable
12     {
13     ⊞         ...void Dispose();
15     }
16     }
```

Figure 22.1.11: The definition of IDisposable

If you expand `public interface IDisposable`, it displays the comment, **Performs application-defined tasks associated with freeing, releasing or resetting unmanaged resources**; in other words, these are low-level resources, so stick to not using this.

Also, you want to confirm that it saves to the file, so enter the following under `using System.IO;`, near the top of the file:

```
using System.Diagnostics;
```

This line will open Notepad after everything has been saved.

Now, below the closed curly brace under `sampLabel.Text = ex.Message;`, enter the following:

```
Process.Start("notepad.exe", TextBox1.Text);
```

Here, `TextBox1.Text` just feeds back the text that you enter in the box.

For the next stage, go back into `Default.aspx`. In the **Design** view, double-click on the **Open In Page** button. This will again take you into `Default.aspx.cs`. The next code that you write will be performed on the `Open` button. So it's very similar in logic.

Now, beneath the open curly brace, under the line that begins with `protected void Button1_Click...`, enter the following:

```
try
{
}
catch(Exception ex)
{
    sampLabel.Text = ex.Message;
}
```

Again, you use `try` and then `catch`, because errors could be generated when you try to open. Display the same text on the label. Basically, take the `try`/`catch` block from above and copy it and paste it down below. It's exactly the same thing.

Creating a StreamReader class

Now, however, you'll enter the following between the set of curly braces under this `try` statement:

```
using (StreamReader sr = new StreamReader(TextBox1.Text))
```

Again, `StreamReader` is a class—it needs a stream. A *stream* is like a channel of communication between two places.

Next, to display the text, enter the following between a set of curly braces below this line:

```
sampLabel.Text = sr.ReadToEnd();
```

Here, `ReadToEnd` is a function available inside the `StreamReader` class, and it reads all of the characters from the current position to the end of the stream. This is sufficient for our purposes. So this is the code.

You've created the simple interface that you can see in the **Design** view, as shown previously in *Figure 22.1.7*.

Running the program

Now, crank it up in in your browser. At the top, you have **Save Path**. First, imagine that no path is entered in the box and you click on the **Save** button. As you can see in *Figure 22.1.12*, it opens Notepad; so, that portion works. However, it displays the message **Empty path name is not legal.** But that's a useful thing, correct?

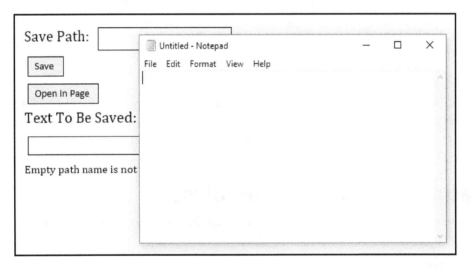

Figure 22.1.12: With no path specified, an error message is displayed and a blank Notepad opens

Now, let's specify a legal path, say `c:\data\temp.txt`. Then, enter `Big Project` in the **Text To Be Saved** box. Click on the **Save** button. **Big Project** is opened and the file is called **temp**, as shown in *Figure 22.1.13*. So, it's been saved:

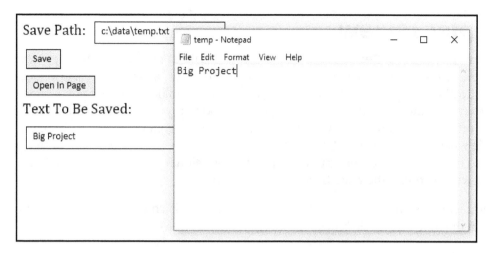

Figure 22.1.13: With a legal path specified, Notepad opens showing the text from the Text To Be Saved box

If you want, you can confirm that it will open in the page, so click on **Open In Page**, and it also now says **Big Project** in the page, as shown in *Figure 22.1.14*:

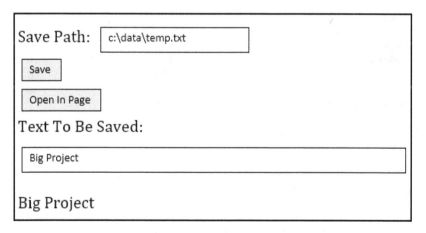

Figure 22.1.14: The text is also opened in the page

So, it's working as expected.

Chapter review

To review, go back into `Default.aspx.cs`. Because you are working with input/output resources, you have to make sure that you have I/O (`using System.IO;`); also, because you are dealing with low-level disk writing and reading, make sure that you enclose `StreamWriter` and `StreamReader` within `using`, so that you can get them, use them, and dispose off them properly. Lastly, because it's common to generate an exception, for example when the path cannot be found or similar, also, use `try` and `catch` with a message shown to the user to make the application look professional. Remember, this will run because we're running the page from our local computer.

The complete version of the `Default.aspx.cs` file for this chapter, including comments, is shown in the following code block:

```
//using is a directive
//System is a name space
//name space is a collection of features that our needs to run
using System;
using System.IO;//needed for files
using System.Diagnostics;//needed for Process.Start
//public means accessible anywhere
//partial means this class is split over multiple files
//class is a keyword and think of it as the outermost level of grouping
//:System.Web.UI.Page means our page inherits the features of a Page
public partial class _Default : System.Web.UI.Page
{
    protected void Button2_Click(object sender, EventArgs e)
    {
        //this is needed so that errors can be caught
        try
        {
            //enclose Streams inside usings because streams deal with
            //low level access
            using (StreamWriter sw = new StreamWriter(TextBox1.Text))
            {
                //this writes the text to a file
                sw.Write(TextBox2.Text);
            }
        }
        catch(Exception ex)
        {
            sampLabel.Text = ex.Message;
        }
        Process.Start("notepad.exe", TextBox1.Text);
    }
    protected void Button1_Click(object sender, EventArgs e)
```

```
    {
        //same as try above
        try
        {
            //save as StreamWriter above
            using (StreamReader sr = new StreamReader(TextBox1.Text))
            {
                //read file contents into label text property
                sampLabel.Text = sr.ReadToEnd();
            }
        }
        catch (Exception ex)
        {
            sampLabel.Text = ex.Message;
        }
    }
}
```

Summary

In this chapter, you learned how to make a page and then save stuff from the page to a hard drive and read it back. You created a simple user interface, created the code to catch an exception, and created the `StreamWriter` and `StreamReader` classes.

In the next chapter, you will learn how to use the Upload feature in ASP.NET.

23

Creating a Page That Uses the File Upload Control

In this chapter, you will learn how to use the Upload feature in ASP.NET. To do this, we will create an interface with the following controls on the page:

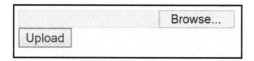

Figure 23.2.1: The controls for our user interface

When you click on the **Browse** button, you should get some sample files, as shown in *Figure 23.2.2*. Select one of these files, for example, samp.txt:

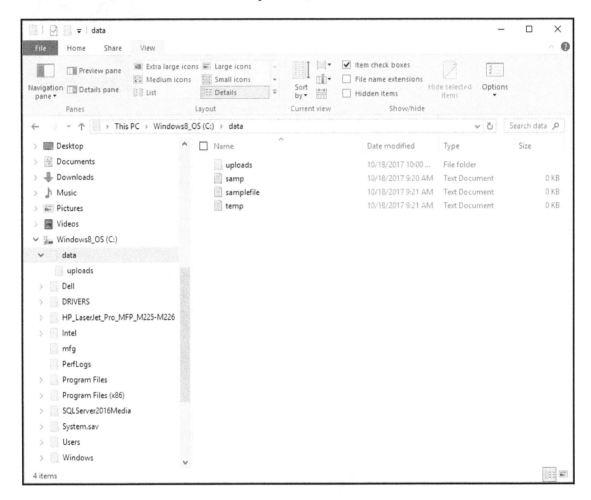

Figure 23.2.2: The C:\data directory file listing

Now, when you click on the **Upload** button, and once the file is uploaded, browser will display a message like the one shown in *Figure 23.2.3*, displaying where the files have been uploaded, how many files are inside the directory, and what they are named. This is our objective here:

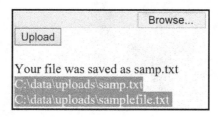

Figure 23.2.3: Message displayed when the Upload button is clicked

Make sure that you have data as a folder in the root directory of your hard drive, and within that folder, you have another folder called uploads. To do this at the command-line level, go to Command Prompt (C:\) and follow these steps:

1. Type cd.. to change to the root directory.
2. Then, type cd data and press *Enter*.
3. At the C:\data directory, type dir, as follows:

C:\data\dir

4. At the C:\data directory, type cd uploads, as follows:

C:\data\cd uploads

5. At the C:\data\uploads directory, type dir again:

C:\data\cd uploads\dir

Your screen will look similar to the one shown in *Figure 23.2.4*:

```
C:\>cd data

C:\data>dir
 Volume in drive C is Windows8_OS
 Volume Serial Number is FEFC-D27F

 Directory of C:\data

10/18/2017  10:00 AM    <DIR>          .
10/18/2017  10:00 AM    <DIR>          ..
10/18/2017  09:20 AM                 0 samp.txt
10/18/2017  09:21 AM                 0 samplefile.txt
10/18/2017  09:21 AM                 0 temp.txt
10/18/2017  10:00 AM    <DIR>          uploads
               3 File(s)              0 bytes
               3 Dir(s)   54,443,655,168 bytes free

C:\data>cd uploads

C:\data\uploads>dir
 Volume in drive C is Windows8_OS
 Volume Serial Number is FEFC-D27F

 Directory of C:\data\uploads

10/18/2017  10:00 AM    <DIR>          .
10/18/2017  10:00 AM    <DIR>          ..
               0 File(s)              0 bytes
               2 Dir(s)   54,443,655,168 bytes free

C:\data\uploads>
```

Figure 23.2.4: Command line directory listing of C:\data\uploads

Now let's make this happen.

Starting our project from scratch

Let's make a new project from scratch. Go to **File | New | Web Site...**; then, go to **Solution Explorer** and click on `Default.aspx`.

We can now see a basic HTML. Let's place a `FileUpload` control into it. To do this, go to **Toolbox**, grab a `FileUpload` control, and drag and drop it below the line that begins with `<form id=...`, and add a `<br/>` tag to it, as follows:

```
<asp:FileUploadID ="FileUpload1" runat="server" /><br/>
```

Next, let's put in a button underneath this line, as follows:

```
<asp:Button ID="Button1" runat="server" Text="Upload" /><br />
```

Change the text on the button so that it says something more meaningful, such as Upload.

Delete the two `<div>` lines—you won't need them.

When you go to the **Design** view, you have this simple interface, as shown in *Figure 23.2.5*. You have a **Browse** button, which is part of the upload control, so that it doesn't have to be put in there separately, and an **Upload** button:

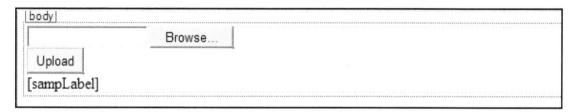

Figure 23.2.5: The simple interface for our project

Now, double-click on the **Upload** button. This takes you into Default.aspx.cs. Delete the Page_Load block. The relevant portion of the starting code for this project should look like *Figure 23.2.6*:

```
1      using System;
2
3      public partial class _Default : System.Web.UI.Page
4      {
5          protected void Button1_Click(object sender, EventArgs e)
6          {
7
8          }
9      }
10
```

Figure 23.2.6: The starting code for this project

Adding a namespace

For reading files, begin by inserting the following after `using System` near the top of the file:

```
using System.IO;
```

Saving a file to a specific location

The first thing that you need to do is to specify a place where files should be saved. So, enter the following between a set of curly braces under the line that begins with `protected void Button1_Click...`:

```
string savePath = @"c:\data\uploads\";
```

Here, `savePath` is the name of the path where file will be saved. You enter the @ symbol to make a verbatim string, and `c:\data\uploads` is where it will be saved. Keep in mind that if you remove the @ symbol it results in errors, because it means read the string exactly as it is.

Next, enter the following:

```
if(FileUpload1.HasFile)
```

Here, `HasFile` is a simple property. Then, you can say the following (between a set of curly braces):

```
{
    string fileName = FileUpload1.FileName;
}
```

This line gets the filename, and here again, `FileName` is a property.

Now, enter the following:

```
savePath += fileName;
```

So, `savePath` begins by being the folder structure, and then you also attach to it the filename.

Saving the file

Now, to actually save the file, enter the following:

```
FileUpload1.SaveAs(savePath);
```

Remember, anytime you want to learn more about any of these terms, you can do so. Just right-click on them and select **Go To Definition**. For example, as shown in *Figure 23.2.7*, if you expand the `public void SaveAs` line, it says **Saves the contents of an uploaded file to specified path on the Web server**. Also, it throws exceptions, so there is the possibility of errors. Keep that in mind.

```
112      //
113      // Summary:
114      //     Saves the contents of an uploaded file to a specified path on the Web server.
115      //
116      // Parameters:
117      //   filename:
118      //     A string that specifies the full path of the location of the server on which
119      //     to save the uploaded file.
120      //
121      // Exceptions:
122      //   T:System.Web.HttpException:
123      //       filename is not a full path.
124      public void SaveAs(string filename);
```

Figure 23.2.7: The explanation of SaveAs within Go To Definition

Displaying messages to the user

Next, let's display some useful diagnostic messages to the user. To do this, enter the following:

```
sampLabel.Text = "<br>Your file was saved as " + fileName;
```

The other possibility is that there is no file. So, in other words, `FileUpload1.HasFile` is false. If that's the case—there's no file, you can take the preceding line, paste it down below, and change the text so that it makes sense. Start by typing `else` below the preceding closing brace, and then enter the following:

```
{
    sampLabel.Text = "<br>You did not specify a file to upload.";
}
```

Determining which files are stored in a directory

Next, let's go and see what files are inside the directory. So, enter the following below the closing brace underneath the preceding line:

```
string sourceDirectory = @"C:\data\uploads";
```

Again, you'll get it from the same place as in the earlier line that begins with `String savePath...`, and paste `c:\data\uploads\` in this line here.

Next, you start by typing `try` on the line that follows, and between a set of curly braces under that, enter this:

```
{
    var txtFiles = Directory.EnumerateFiles(sourceDirectory, "*.txt");
}
```

The tooltip that appears while entering `EnumerateFiles` says that there are a couple of overloads—`string path` and `string searchPattern`. So, here the path will be `sourceDirectory`, and `searchPattern` will be used to search for everything ending with `.txt`. Hence we put `*.txt` at the end. This is how you can enumerate all of the files.

Determining the return type

If you hover your mouse over `var` in the preceding line, the pop-up tooltip tells you what the return type is. It says `IEnumerable`. Now hover your mouse over `EnumerateFiles`, right-click on it, and select **Go To Definition**:

```
23    public static IEnumerable<string> EnumerateDirectories(string path);
24    public static IEnumerable<string> EnumerateDirectories(string path, string searchPattern);
25    public static IEnumerable<string> EnumerateDirectories(string path, string searchPattern, SearchOption searchOption);
26    public static IEnumerable<string> EnumerateFiles(string path);
27    public static IEnumerable<string> EnumerateFiles(string path, string searchPattern);
28    public static IEnumerable<string> EnumerateFiles(string path, string searchPattern, SearchOption searchOption);
29    public static IEnumerable<string> EnumerateFileSystemEntries(string path);
30    public static IEnumerable<string> EnumerateFileSystemEntries(string path, string searchPattern, SearchOption searchOption);
31    public static IEnumerable<string> EnumerateFileSystemEntries(string path, string searchPattern);
```

Figure 23.2.8: In the definition, it shows that the return type is IEnumerable

As shown in *Figure 23.2.8*, the return type is `IEnumerable`, which means that you can iterate over the results, or display them using a `foreach` statement.

Next, enter the following beneath the preceding line:

```
foreach(string currentFile in txtFiles)
```

Then just below this, enter the following (indented):

```
sampLabel.Text += $"<br>{currentFile}";
```

Exploring the exceptions for EnumerateFiles

Now, again hold your mouse over `EnumerateFiles`, right-click on it, and select **Go To Definition**. Expand the definition and look at the exceptions that it can throw. There are quite a few of them, a sampling of which is shown in *Figure 23.2.9*:

```
393    //   T:System.IO.DirectoryNotFoundException:
394    //       path is invalid, such as referring to an unmapped drive.
395    //
396    //   T:System.IO.IOException:
397    //       path is a file name.
398    //
399    //   T:System.IO.PathTooLongException:
400    //       The specified path, file name, or combined exceed the system-defined maximum
401    //       length. For example, on Windows-based platforms, paths must be less than 248
402    //       characters and file names must be less than 260 characters.
403    //
404    //   T:System.Security.SecurityException:
405    //       The caller does not have the required permission.
```

Figure 23.2.9: A partial listing of the exceptions that EnumerateFiles can throw

As an example, `DirectoryNotFound` might be a common exception; `path` is a filename, `PathTooLong` and `SecurityException` are also common exceptions. So, there are quite a few for `EnumerateFiles`.

Catching the exceptions

In other words, you need to insert some kind of `catch` to handle these things. So, enter the following after the last closed curly brace:

```
catch(Exception ex)
```

Now, between a set of curly braces, enter the following:

```
{
    sampLabel.Text += ex.Message;
}
```

Here, `ex.Message` represents the message from the exception object to be displayed on the screen.

Running the program

Now let's confirm that this will work, so crank it up in your browser. Click on **Browse**, and grab the `temp.txt` file from the `C:\data` directory. Click on **Upload**. As you can see in *Figure 23.2.10*, your file has been saved, and there are the other files in that same directory. Perfect!

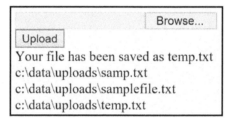

Figure 23.2.10: The results of running our program

Now, imagine that you made an error like the following (typing `upload` instead of *uploads*):

```
string sourceDirectory = @"C:\data\upload";
```

If you run it again, by clicking on **Browse** and selecting the `samplefile.txt` file, you can see from the error message shown in *Figure 23.2.11* that it **Could not find a part of the path...** :

Figure 23.2.11: Error message displayed when the path is incorrectly entered

So these are the basics of making this work. Again, be sure to enter and run this code a few times, and then you'll know exactly what's going on. Remember, we can do this safely because the web page is accessible only on our local computer. In a more realistic situation, you would need to be more concerned with security and guard against malicious uploads.

Chapter review

The complete version of the `Default.aspx.cs` file for this chapter, including comments, is shown in the following code block:

```
using System;
using System.IO;
public partial class _Default : System.Web.UI.Page
{
    protected void Button1_Click(object sender, EventArgs e)
    {
        string savePath = @"c:\data\uploads\"; //make upload directory
        if (FileUpload1.HasFile)
        {
            string fileName = FileUpload1.FileName;//get file name
            savePath += fileName;//attach file name to save path
            FileUpload1.SaveAs(savePath);//save file
            sampLabel.Text = "<br>Your file was saved as " + fileName;
        }
        else
        {
            sampLabel.Text = "<br>You did not specify a file to upload.";
        }
        //could also use savePath here
        string sourceDirectory = @"C:\data\uploads";
        try
        {
            //list files using EnumerateFiles
            var txtFiles = Directory.EnumerateFiles(sourceDirectory,
            "*.txt");
            foreach (string currentFile in txtFiles) //display files
            sampLabel.Text += $"<br>{currentFile}";
        }
        //display any error messages
        catch (Exception ex)
        {
            sampLabel.Text += ex.Message;
        }
    }
}
```

Summary

In this chapter, you learned how to use the Upload feature in ASP.NET. You saved a file to a specific location, displayed messages to the user, determined which files are stored in a directory, explored the exceptions for `EnumerateFiles`, and wrote the code to catch the exceptions.

In the next chapter, you will learn another way of saving objects with the hard drive using serialization. Then, you will learn about the process of rebuilding an object from the hard drive, which is called **deserialization**.

24

Serializing and Deserializing Objects

In this chapter, you will learn another way of saving objects to a hard drive—using serialization. You will also learn the process of rebuilding an object from the hard drive, which is called deserialization.

Adding two buttons to the HTML

Crank up a project, and in this one, you will insert two buttons into the **<html>** page. You'll place the first button below the line beginning with <form id=.... To do this, go to **Toolbox**, grab a Button control, and drag it in there. Change the text on the first button to say Save. Now grab another button, and drag and drop it below that line. Change the text on the second button to say Open. So you place two buttons in the page, as follows:

```
<asp:ButtonID="Button1" runat="server" Text="Save" /><br/>
<asp:ButtonID="Button2" runat="server" Text="Open" /><br/>
```

Delete the two <div> lines—you won't need them. Of course, at the end you also have a label:

```
<asp:LabelID="sampLabel" runat="server"></asp:Label>
```

In the **Design** view, as shown in *Figure 24.3.1*, you have two buttons—**Save** and **Open**—and then a label where the opened object can be displayed:

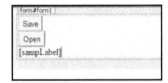

Figure 24.3.1: Our simple interface in the Design view

Beginning to code the project

First, we will create the `Save` button, so double-click on it, which brings up the event handler for `Button1_click`. Delete the `Page_Load` block. The relevant portion of the starting code for this project should look like *Figure 24.3.2*:

```
1   //using is a directive
2   //System is a name space
3   //name space is a collection of features that our needs to run
4   using System;
5                       //public means accessible anywhere
6                       //partial means this class is split over multiple files
7                       //class is a keyword and think of it as the outermost level of grouping
8                       //:System.Web.UI.Page means our page inherits the features of a Page
9   public partial class _Default : System.Web.UI.Page
10  {
11      protected void Button1_Click(object sender, EventArgs e)
12      {
13
14      }
15  }
16
```

Figure 24.3.2: The starting code for this project

Adding namespaces

Next, you need to add new namespaces, so near the top of the file under `using System`, enter the following:

```
using System.IO;
```

Clearly, this line is used for input and output. Next, enter the following:

```
using System.Runtime.Serialization.Formatters.Binary;
```

This line allows you to do the write of the code. You'll understand the purpose of these namespaces better as we write the code together. Next, let's do one more, as follows:

```
using System.Diagnostics;
```

This line is needed just so that you can open Notepad. You will use Notepad to view the file after it's saved in binary format. Now you can collapse these namespaces if you like.

Creating a serializable class

So first you need something that you can serialize—a serializable class. You will place that below that previous `using` statement. Enter the following:

```
[Serializable()]
```

You can decorate a class this way. Next, the thing to be serialized is entered below this, as follows:

```
public class Person
```

Adding features to the serializable class

This is your serializable class. Next, you will add features to it. So, between a set of curly braces beneath this line, enter the following:

```
public string Name { get; set; }
public decimal Salary { get; set; }
```

Next, we will override a method so that we can display a person and actually format it. So, enter the following:

```
public override string ToString()
```

Now, if you hover your mouse over `ToString`, you'll see that it's an object class. Remember, an object class is the parent class of the entire hierarchy. This is where `ToString` is defined. The tooltip says **string object.ToString()**. We'll now overwrite it and write our own definition.

Next, enter the following between a set of curly braces beneath the `override` line:

```
return $"{Name} makes {Salary:C} per year.";
```

This will be our particular implementation of `ToString`; that is, `Name` makes some amount of money per year—whatever the name and salary happen to be for each instance of the `Person` class.

Defining the path for saving a file

Next, within a set of curly braces beneath the line that begins with `protected void Button1_Click...`, enter the following:

```
string file = @"c:\data\person.bin";
```

Here, you're defining the path where the file will be saved. Note that this time we are using a different extension—`.bin` for binary, rather than `.txt` for text.

Making a Person object

Next, to make a new `Person` object, enter the following:

```
Person per = new Person() { Name = "John Smith", Salary = 78999 };
```

Remember, another way of creating objects is that you can set the values of the properties within curly braces. So here we have `John Smith` and his `Salary` property value. Thus, we've made a `new Person` object.

Handling unmanaged resources

Now, enter the following:

```
using (FileStream str = File.Create(file))
```

Hover your mouse over `FileStream` in the preceding line to see where it's located; it's inside `System.IO`. Notice that `using System.IO;` is no longer greyed out because `FileStream` is now there.

Next, right-click on `FileStream` and select **Go To Definition**. You can see that it is derived from `Stream`. Now, if you scroll down to the bottom where it says `Dispose` and expand that, you'll see that it says **Releases the unmanaged resources used by the System.IO.FileStream...**, as shown in *Figure 24.3.3*:

```
1461        //
1462        // Summary:
1463        //     Releases the unmanaged resources used by the System.IO.FileStream and optionally
1464        //     releases the managed resources.
1465        //
1466        // Parameters:
1467        //   disposing:
1468        //     true to release both managed and unmanaged resources; false to release only unmanaged
1469        //     resources.
1470        [SecuritySafeCritical]
1471        protected override void Dispose(bool disposing);
1472    }
1473 }
```

Figure 24.3.3: Expanded definition of FileStream

This is why we put it inside a `using` statement, because it deals with unmanaged resources, such as low-level disk access. So, we will create a file.

Making a binary formatter

Next, you'll make a binary formatter, so enter the following between a set of curly braces:

```
BinaryFormatter binFormatter = new BinaryFormatter();
```

Again, `BinaryFormatter` here is a class, so if you hover your mouse over it, the tooltip says **Serializes and deserializes an object, or an entire graph of connected objects in binary format.**

Serializing an object

Next, to serialize our object, you say `binFormatter.Serialize`, which is a function defined there, and then you need a stream and an object (`per`) to be serialized through the stream:

```
binFormatter.Serialize(str, per);
```

To confirm that this works, enter the following below the closing curly brace:

```
Process.Start("notepad.exe", file);
```

This will just launch the file for us to confirm that it's been saved.

Testing the program

Before we write the rest of the code, we can give this one a test. So let's launch this in a browser and click on **Save**:

Figure 24.3.4: A test run of the program to make sure that it works

You can see now that when you examine it, the stuff that was saved looks very different from just plain text. Remember that when you were learning about properties, we talked about *backing fields*. The actual value of the fields is shown in *Figure 24.3.5*. You can see the salary, the name values, and then the fields. This is what we mean by *binary*. It looks quite different from just plain text:

Figure 24.3.5: The Backing Field shows the actual values of the field

Rebuilding an object from a hard drive

In the next stage, we want to be able to rebuild this object from the hard drive. For this, double-click on the **Open** button in the **Design** view. This takes you back into the `Default.aspx.cs` file.

Now, within a set of curly braces below the line that begins with `protected void Button2_Click...`, you'll make a new `Person` object, as follows:

```
Person personRebuilt;
```

We construct this from the hard drive. Next, enter the following below this line:

```
string file = @"c:\data\person.bin";
```

With this line, we'll be reading back from that file.

Next, you have to confirm that the file actually exists, so enter the following:

```
if(File.Exists(file))
```

If the file exists, you will take some actions, and those actions will be the ones that rebuild the objects.

Now enter the following between a set of curly braces below this line:

```
using (FileStream personStream = File.OpenRead(file))
```

Here, we open the file for reading. Hover your mouse over OpenRead. Notice that it returns a FileStream class, so the right-hand and left-hand sides of the expression agree.

Next, between another set of curly braces below this line, enter the following:

```
BinaryFormatter binReader = new BinaryFormatter();
```

Now, we will rebuild the Person object, so enter the following next:

```
personRebuilt = (Person)binReader.Deserialize(personStream);
```

This will be a cast to the Person type. Then, you're passing in personStream into the Deserialize function, defined on the binary reader, and then you cast that back up to a Person object.

Displaying the results

Now, with that in place we can display things. For example, enter the following next:

```
sampLabel.Text = personRebuilt.ToString();
```

Remember that ToString in this line is the one that's defined inside Person. It's the one that overrides the basic ToString method defined inside the object. If you hover your mouse over ToString here, it says **string Person.ToString()**.

Running the program

Now let's open this in your browser with this new code in place. Click on the **Save** button, and it opens Notepad, as shown in *Figure 24.3.6*:

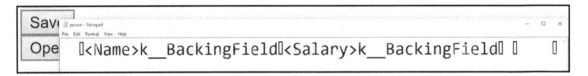

Figure 24.3.6: The results of running the program when the Save button is clicked

Now click on the **Open** button, and it looks like the screen shown in *Figure 24.3.7*:

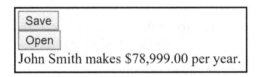

Figure 24.3.7: The results of running the program when the Open button is clicked

So, this proves that the object has been constructed, and it also confirms that on this reconstructed object, `personRebuilt`, you can call the usual functions, methods, and so on, that were spelled out in the definition of the class in the `return $"{Name} makes {Salary:C} per year.";` line.

Chapter review

To review, remember that the big idea here is that you can start with an object and add quite a few namespaces, specifically `BinaryFormatter` and `IO`. Next, you define a class, and add the serializable attribute below. Then you write code to save in a binary format and also code to reconstruct from the binary format to the one that you can use in your app.

The complete version of the `Default.aspx.cs` file for this chapter, including comments, is shown in the following code block:

```
//using is a directive
//System is a name space
//name space is a collection of features that our needs to run
using System;
using System.IO;
using System.Runtime.Serialization.Formatters.Binary;
```

```csharp
using System.Diagnostics; //for notepad
//public means accessible anywhere
//partial means this class is split over multiple files
//class is a keyword and think of it as the outermost level of grouping
//:System.Web.UI.Page means our page inherits the features of a Page
[Serializable()]
public class Person //make class serializable
{
    public string Name { get; set; } //define name property
    public decimal Salary { get; set; } //define Salary property
    public override string ToString()
    //override ToString() from object class
    {
        //return pretty string to describe each person
        return $"{Name} makes {Salary:C} per year.";
    }
}
public partial class _Default : System.Web.UI.Page
{
    protected void Button1_Click(object sender, EventArgs e)
    {
        //define path where file will be saved
        string file = @"c:\data\person.bin";
        //build an object
        Person per = new Person() { Name = "John Smith", Salary = 78999 };
        //enclose FileStream in a using because of low level access
        using (FileStream str = File.Create(file))
        {
            //make a formatter
            BinaryFormatter binFormatter = new BinaryFormatter();
            //this is the step that saves the information
            binFormatter.Serialize(str, per);
        }
        //start notepad and display file
        Process.Start("notepad.exe", file);
    }
    protected void Button2_Click(object sender, EventArgs e)
    {
        //person object to hold the rebuild person from disk
        Person personRebuilt;
        string file = @"c:\data\person.bin"; //path
        if(File.Exists(file)) //first confirm file exists
        {
            //enclose FileStream in a using
            using (FileStream personStream = File.OpenRead(file))
            {
                //make a formatter
                BinaryFormatter binReader = new BinaryFormatter();
```

```
                        //reconstruct person using a cast
                        personRebuilt =
                        (Person)binReader.Deserialize(personStream);
                        //invoke to string on the person
                        sampLabel.Text = personRebuilt.ToString();
                    }
                }
            }
        }
```

Summary

In this chapter, you learned another way of saving objects to the hard drive—using serialization. Then, you learned the process of rebuilding an object from the hard drive—deserialization. You created a `serializable` class, added features to the class, defined the path for saving a file, made a `Person` object, wrote code to handle unmanaged resources, made a binary formatter, serialized an object, and tested your program.

In the next chapter, you will take a look at working with images at the pixel level. We will invert the colors and change that around.

25

Having a Little Fun with Images with Pixel Manipulations

In this chapter, you will learn how to work with images at the pixel level. You will invert the colors, changing them around.

Manipulating an image

To start, in my `c:\data` folder, I have a file called *lessonimage*. As you can see in *Figure 25.4.1*, the writing on the Coke can is red and the background seems to be reddish-brown:

Figure 25.4.1: The image to be used for inverting colors at the pixel level in this chapter

What we will do is switch the colors around, so that the writing on the Coke can, for example, will become green, and you will learn how you can manipulate images at the individual pixel level.

Adding a button and an image control to the HTML

Open up a new project. Delete the two lines that begin with `<div...`; also delete the `Label` line this time. You don't need any of them.

Next, you need to insert a `Button` control into the **<html>** page. To do this, go to **Toolbox**, grab a `Button` control, and drag and drop it below the line beginning with `<form id=....` Change the text on the first button to say `Load`.

Now you need to insert an image control into the **<html>** page. So, go back to **Toolbox**, grab an `Image` control, and drag and drop it below the previous line, leaving a blank line in between the two. Your `Default.aspx` file should look like the one shown in *Figure 25.4.2*:

```
1    <%@ Page Language="C#" AutoEventWireup="true" CodeFile="Default.aspx.cs" Inherits="_Default" %>
2
3    <!DOCTYPE html>
4
5    <html xmlns="http://www.w3.org/1999/xhtml">
6    <head runat="server">
7        <title>Our First Page</title>
8    </head>
9    <body>
10       <form id="form1" runat="server">
11           <asp:Button ID="Button1" runat="server" Text="Load" /><br />
12
13           <asp:Image ID="Image1" runat="server" />
14       </form>
15   </body>
16   </html>
17
```

Figure 25.4.2: The complete HTML for this chapter

So, you have a very simple interface for this project: one button to load an image and the other one, which is an image control, to display the image:

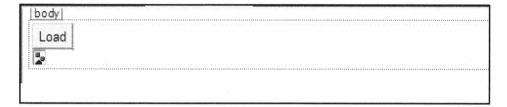

Figure 25.4.3: The simple interface for our project

Now, double-click on the **Load** button. This takes you into `Default.aspx.cs`. Delete the `Page_Load` event; we don't care about that one. The relevant portion of the starting code for this project should look like *Figure 25.4.4*:

```
1    //using is a directive
2    //System is a name space
3    //name space is a collection of features that our needs to run
4    using System;
5    //public means accessible anywhere
6    //partial means this class is split over multiple files
7    //class is a keyword and think of it as the outermost level of grouping
8    //:System.Web.UI.Page means our page inherits the features of a Page
9    public partial class _Default : System.Web.UI.Page
10   {
11       protected void Button1_Click(object sender, EventArgs e)
12       {
13
14       }
15   }
16
```

Figure 25.4.4: The starting code for this project

Adding a namespace

Naturally enough, the first thing to do is to add a new namespace that's relevant. For this, enter the following line under `using System`, near the top of the file:

```
using System.Drawing;
```

To make things nice and clean, you can collapse all of the code groups at the top of the file if you like so that basically the first clearly visible line is `public partial class....`

Making a bitmap

The next stage, of course, is to put in the code that will do what you want to do. First, you will make a bitmap. Enter the following between a set of curly braces below the line that begins with `protected void Button1_Click...`:

```
Bitmap image = new Bitmap(@"c:\data\lessonimage.bmp");
```

Here, `Bitmap` is a class that we will call `image`. Basically, you have a map of bits that can be manipulated. Then, to initialize it, you pass in a path. In this case, it is `(@"c:\data\lessonimage.bmp");`.

Saving an image as a bitmap picture

Next, open **Paint** and load the image to be manipulated in this chapter, as shown in *Figure 25.4.5*:

Figure 25.4.5: The image to be manipulated in Paint

Now, to save it as a bitmap, go to **File | Save As**, and then select **BMP picture**, as shown in *Figure 25.4.6*:

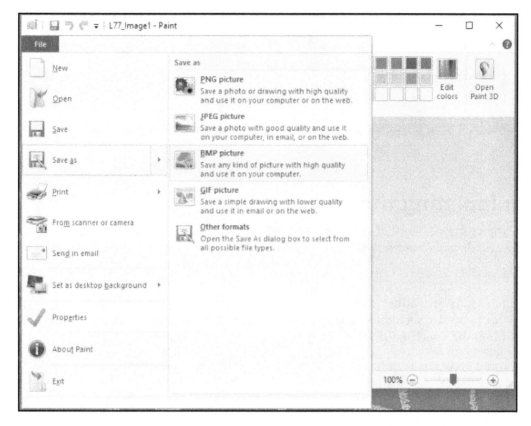

Figure 25.4.6: Save As options in Paint

The description of **BMP picture** says **Save any kind of picture with high quality and use it on your computer.** When you go to save the file, the **Save as type:** field in the **Save As** dialog box says **24-bit bitmap (*.bmp;*.dib)**. You can save any images as a bitmap there.

Accessing a pixel's location

Next, enter the following after `Bitmap image = new Bitmap...` line:

```
int x, y;
```

You need this line to get each pixel's location inside the image.

Now, to access each pixel's location, you need nested `for` loops. Start by entering this line next:

```
for(x = 0; x < image.Width; x++)
```

The outer `for` loop here is for controlling the horizontal movement of the x coordinate.

Now, between a set of curly braces, enter the following:

```
for(y = 0; y < image.Height; y++)
```

This inner `for` loop is needed to control the y coordinate of each pixel, or its vertical position.

Manipulating the pixels

Once you've done all of that, the next stage is to manipulate the pixels. So, start with another set of curly braces, and begin by entering the following, indented, between them:

```
Color pixelColor = image.GetPixel(x, y);
```

This line begins by reading each pixel's color first. If you hover your mouse over `GetPixel` in this line, you will see that it returns a color, not the location. The tooltip says that it **Gets the color of the specified pixel in this Bitmap**.

Now you'll make a new color. Enter the following, also indented, next:

```
Color newColor = Color.FromArgb(pixelColor.B, pixelColor.R, pixelColor.G);
```

Here, `Color` following the = sign is a `struct` value type. In addition to `FromArgb`, you can also use `FromKnownColor` or `FromName`. This means that the string name is known. Following `FromArgb`, you say `pixelColor.B` to get the blue component of this color structure, `pixelColor.R` to get the red component, and then `pixelColor.G` to get the green component. Thus, you make a new `Color` object with this line.

Next, enter the following:

```
image.SetPixel(x, y, newColor);
```

If you hover your mouse over `SetPixel`, the tooltip says **Sets the color of the specified pixel in this Bitmap.** Then, `(x, y, newColor)` represents the new color to be used to color that pixel.

Converting the picture to a byte array

Now you need to be able to display the picture. You need to write some code to accomplish the conversion. So, start by entering the following beneath the closed curly brace of the outer `for` loop:

```
byte[] picBytes = (byte[])new ImageConverter().ConvertTo(image,
typeof(byte[]));
```

Here, you make a byte array, called `picBytes`, then `(byte[])` is used to convert for casting. There's an image converter class, so you make a new `ImageConverter()` class, and then you convert to a destination type, `typeof`, and then `byte`. So, here you convert the picture to a byte array.

Now if you were to remove the `(byte[])` cast, the tooltip would then say that your byte array **Cannot implicitly convert type 'object' to byte[]**. This is the case because `ConvertTo` returns an object. Thus, you need to have that `(byte[])` cast right there in front of it.

Now that you have this, you can say the following next:

```
string baseString = Convert.ToBase64String(picBytes);
```

Inside `Convert`, you can now enter `Convert.ToBase64String`, and `picBytes` can be converted to `base64` string.

Sending out the image URL

Now you can send out the image URL, so enter the following:

```
Image1.ImageUrl = "data:image/png;base64," + baseString;
```

The `baseString` variable at the end of this line is the result of running two `base64` strings on an array of picture bytes.

Running the program

With this in place, now let's take a look at the results; open your browser and click on the **Load** button. The altered image is shown in *Figure 25.4.7*:

Figure 25.4.7: The manipulated image that resulted when the program was run

You'll see now that the picture has been inverted as promised: the colors are green. The background was kind of a reddish-brown in the original, and now it's green. The man's hair was kind of brown and now it's kind of dark, and likewise with the table. Some of the things, however, do not appear to be much affected, like the money color, right? That is still kind of grayish. The same thing with the black objects in the image.

As you can see, you can manipulate images, change them around, and make them look very different, so nothing is really permanently fixed. That's the point. Also, you can access each pixel individually, change the color, and then the last three lines of code in the program are responsible for allowing you to write `Image1.ImageUrl`. To set this image URL, you need to go through the first two lines in that group of three. There could be some simpler ways of doing it, but this is one way that works.

Chapter review

The complete version of the `Default.aspx.cs` file for this chapter, including comments, is shown in the following code block:

```
//using is a directive
//System is a name space
//name space is a collection of features that our needs to run
using System;
using System.Drawing;
//public means accessible anywhere
//partial means this class is split over multiple files
//class is a keyword and think of it as the outermost level of grouping
//:System.Web.UI.Page means our page inherits the features of a Page
public partial class _Default : System.Web.UI.Page
{
    protected void Button1_Click(object sender, EventArgs e)
    {
        Bitmap image = new Bitmap(@"c:\data\lessonimage.bmp");
        //to get each pixel's location
        int x, y;
        //controls moving horizontally
        for(x=0;x<image.Width;x++)
        {
            //controls moving vertically
            for(y=0;y<image.Height;y++)
            {
                //get each pixel's color
                Color pixelColor = image.GetPixel(x, y);
                //make a new color
                Color newColor = Color.FromArgb(pixelColor.B, pixelColor.R,
                pixelColor.G);
                image.SetPixel(x, y, newColor);//set new color
            }
        }
        //converts picture to array of bytes
        byte[] picBytes =(byte[])new ImageConverter().ConvertTo(image,
        typeof(byte[]));
        //converts array of bytes to a certain kind of string
        string baseString = Convert.ToBase64String(picBytes);
        //sets the image URL in a format that allows the image to be
        //displayed in a web page
        Image1.ImageUrl = "data:image/png;base64," + baseString;
    }
}
```

Summary

In this chapter, you learned how to work with images at the pixel level. You inverted the colors, changing them around. You inserted a button and image control into the HTML, made a bitmap, saved an image as a bitmap picture, wrote the code to access each pixel's location to manipulate the pixels, converted the picture to a byte array, and sent out the image URL.

In the next chapter, you will learn how to read files and then save them to SQL Server as images.

26

Saving an Image to SQL Server

In this chapter, you will learn how to read files and then save them in SQL Server as images.

Adding buttons and a list box to HTML

Bring up a project which contains the basic HTML. The first thing that you need to do here is to insert a button. To do this, go to **Toolbox** and drag and drop a `Button` control below the line beginning with `<form id=`.... Remember, the simple interface that we will build in this project will involve clicking on a button and reading files into a list box from your hard drive. Change the text on the `Button` control to say `Scan Folder`. You will scan a folder for images in this project.

After that, you'll insert a `ListBox` control. So again, go to **Toolbox**, type in `list` in the search field, and drag and drop the `ListBox` control below the previous line. You will fill the `ListBox` control after you click on the button.

In the last stage, you will save all of the files to SQL Server. This is our objective. For this, drag in one more button below the preceding line. Change the text on the `Button` control to say `Save To SQL Server`.

Delete the two lines that begin with `<div`..., and also delete the `Label` line again this time. You don't need any of these.

Your `Default.aspx` file should look like the one shown in *Figure 26.5.1*:

```
1    <%@ Page Language="C#" AutoEventWireup="true" CodeFile="Default.aspx.cs" Inherits="_Default" %>
2
3    <!DOCTYPE html>
4
5    <html xmlns="http://www.w3.org/1999/xhtml">
6    <head runat="server">
7        <title>Our First Page</title>
8    </head>
9    <body>
10       <form id="form1" runat="server">
11           <asp:Button ID="Button1" runat="server" Text="Scan Folder" /><br />
12           <asp:ListBox ID="ListBox1" runat="server" Width="273px"></asp:ListBox><br />
13           <asp:Button ID="Button2" runat="server" Text="Save To SQL Server" Width="271px" />
14       </form>
15   </body>
16   </html>
17
```

Figure 26.5.1: The complete HTML for this chapter

Go to the **Design** view, and as shown in *Figure 26.5.2*, you have a very simple interface for this project: a **Scan Folder** button, which gets the filenames, and then a button to save the files to SQL Server:

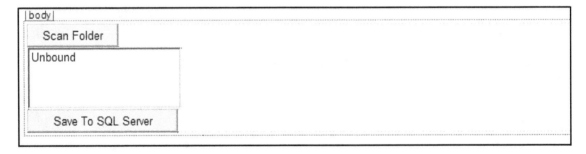

Figure 26.5.2: The simple interface for our project

Creating a database table to store the files

You need to have a database table where the files can be saved. Start by opening **SQL Server Object Explorer**. You'll recall that you've got a database called `People`. Go to the **Tables** folder, right-click on it, and select `Add New Table...`, as shown in *Figure 26.5.3*:

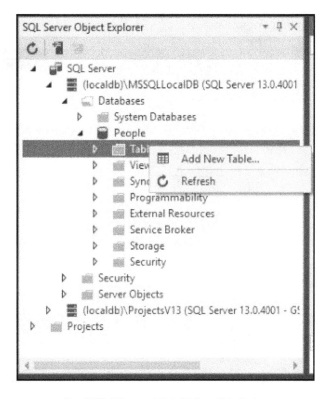

Figure 26.5.3: Adding a new table in SQL Server Object Explorer

You can keep the default stuff at the top pretty much as it is, but make the following changes:

1. Change the first line in the **T-SQL** tab at the bottom, as follows:

```
[Id] INT NOT NULL PRIMARY KEY identity(1.1),
```

2. Add this line next:

```
IMAGE image not null
```

3. Change the name of the table to `Images`, as follows:

```
CREATE TABLE[dbo].Images
```

This is our table, as shown in *Figure 26.5.4*:

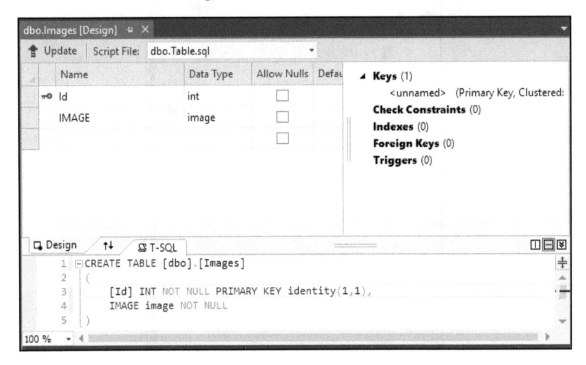

Figure 26.5.4: The dbo.Images table in SQL Server

Let's update this, then, click on the **Update Database** button in the dialog box that appears. Wait for the changes to take effect. So, if you expand the **Tables** node, you should see a **dbo.Images** table with an **IMAGE** column, as shown in *Figure 26.5.5*:

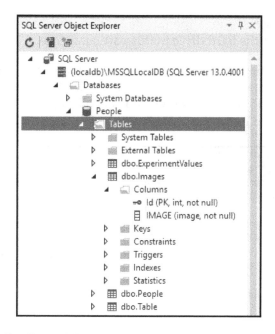

Figure 26.5.5: The Tables node contains the dbo.Images table with an IMAGE column

Storing image files on your hard drive

In the next stage of the process, you have to make sure that you have images to read. So, place a few images somewhere on your `C:\` drive. For example, *Figure 26.5.6* shows the listing obtained when the `dir *.jpeg` command is run against the `C:\data` directory on this particular computer:

```
C:\>cd data

C:\data>dir *.jpeg
 Volume in drive C is Windows8_OS
 Volume Serial Number is FEFC-D27F

 Directory of C:\data

10/21/2017  10:35 AM           160,481 face1.jpeg
10/21/2017  10:37 AM            23,844 face2.jpeg
10/21/2017  10:36 AM           103,410 face3.jpeg
               3 File(s)        287,735 bytes
               0 Dir(s)  53,195,374,592 bytes free

C:\data>
```

Figure 26.5.6: Listing of three images files stored in the C:\data directory

The list shows these images: `face1.jpeg`, `face2.jpeg`, and `face3.jpeg`. So, there are three files to be read from the hard drive in this particular case.

Now double-click on the **Scan Folder** button in the **Design** view. This takes you into `Default.aspx.cs`. Delete the `Page_Load` stub. We will handle the event that comes along with this. There's a fair amount of code involved, so it is more of a project. The relevant portion of the starting code for this project should look like *Figure 26.5.7*:

```
1    //using is a directive
2    //System is a name space
3    //name space is a collection of features that our needs to run
4    using System;
5    //public means accessible anywhere
6    //partial means this class is split over multiple files
7    //class is a keyword and think of it as the outermost level of grouping
8    //:System.Web.UI.Page means our page inherits the features of a Page
9    public partial class _Default : System.Web.UI.Page
10   {
11       protected void Button1_Click(object sender, EventArgs e)
12       {
13
14       }
15   }
16
```

Figure 26.5.7: The starting code for this project

Adding namespaces

First of all, you need to add namespaces that are relevant. So, under `using System` near the top of the file, enter the following:

```
using System.Data.SqlClient;
```

Remember, we use this in connections and commands.
Next, type the following underneath this line:

```
using System.IO;
```

Again, this line is there to be able to read the hard drive. So, these are the two new namespaces. You can now collapse everything above the line that begins with `public partial class....`

Coding the application

Now let's go through the creation of the code line by line. So, starting with the line that begins with `protected void Button1_Click...`, enter the following between a set of curly braces:

```
var imgFiles = Directory.GetFiles(@"c:\data\", "*.jpg");
```

Here, you have a `Directory` class and a file reading method called `GetFiles`, which returns an array of strings that are the paths of the files. Then you specify the path of the directory where they search, so (`@"c:\data\"...`), and then you want to search for image files only, so you can specify a filter, or `*.jpg` in this case. If you hover your mouse over `var`, you can see that it's an array of strings.

Now you can load into the `ListBox` control. Enter the following next:

```
foreach(var imgFile in imgFiles)
```

Next, for each file inside the array of files, enter the following between a set of curly braces:

```
ListBox1.Items.Add(imgFile);
```

So, you get all the file paths, and then, using the `foreach` loop, you add them to the `ListBox` control so that they can be displayed in the page. This is our objective.

Testing the *scanning the folder* function

Go to the **Design** view, and at this point, scanning the folder should work. For this, click on the **Scan Folder** button.

As you can see in *Figure 26.5.8*, the files are loaded:

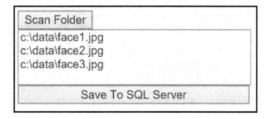

Figure 26.5.8: The files are properly loaded in ListBox

Now that this is complete, you can take each file, again using a `foreach` loop, and save it to SQL Server. Let's do that next.

Building the connection string

Now double-click on the **Save to SQL Server** button in the **Design** view. This takes you back into `Default.aspx.cs`. As you might imagine, the next stage will be to get the connection string. You've done this before. So, within a set of curly braces below the line that begins with `protected void Button2_Click...` , start by entering `string connString =`, followed by the @ symbol to make it a verbatim string, and then you put the `""` symbols. Now to get the connection string, do the following:

1. Click on **View** in the menu bar, and select **SQL Server Object Explorer**.
2. Right-click on the **People** database, and select **Properties**.
3. In the **Properties** pane, double-click on **Connection String** to select it with its long description.
4. Then, right-click on the long description and copy it.
5. Paste the description between the set of the `""` symbols.

The connection string line should then look like the following:

```
string connString = @"Data Source=(localdb)\MSSQLLocalDB;Initial
Catalog=People;Integrated Security=True;Connect
Timeout=30;Encrypt=False;TrustServerCertificate=True;ApplicationIntent=Read
Write;MultiSubnetFailover=False";
```

You can break this over multiple lines so that it's a little neater, if you like. You can now close the **SQL Server Object Explorer** and **Properties** panes.

Using of the connection string

Now we will make use of connection string, of course. So, for the next stage, enter the following:

```
using (SqlConnection conn = new SqlConnection(connString))
```

We'll call connection string `conn`, and `SqlConnection` is initialized with the connection string.

Next, we need to open a connection. Enter the following between a set of curly braces beneath the preceding line:

```
conn.Open();
```

Then, enter the following `foreach` loop:

```
foreach(var item in ListBox1.Items)
```

Here, `Items` is a property of the `ListBox` control. It's a list of the items that it contains, and you can examine them individually so that you can take discrete actions on them. Enter the following within another set of curly braces next:

```
using (SqlCommand cmd = new SqlCommand("insert into dbo.Images (image)
values(@image)", conn))
```

Notice that we're putting `SqlCommand` in a `using` statement. If you right-click on `SqlCommand` and select **Go To Definition**, you'll see that it says, **DbCommand inherits from it**, and if you scroll down to the bottom, you'll see that it has a `Dispose` line. To finish the code here, you have `(image)` as the field, and its parameter is `@image`.

For the next stage, enter the following within another set of curly braces:

```
byte[] picAsBytes = File.ReadAllBytes(item.ToString());
```

If you left the preceding line at just `(item)`, it gives an error underlined in red. So we convert it to `ToString`. Here, we take each item, read it as a sequence of bytes, and store it inside an array, because then, that can be converted into an image in SQL Server.

Enter the following next:

```
cmd.Parameters.AddWithValue("@image", picAsBytes);
```

Again, `@image` here is the parameter. So, we will save the picture to the `image` parameter as a sequence of bytes. Now enter the following:

```
cmd.ExecuteNonQuery();
```

This line performs the actual saving. This, believe it or not, is the entire application.

Running the program

Now let's take a look at the results in your browser. First, click on **Scan Folder**. You can see the list of images. Then, click on the **Save To SQL Server** button. Nothing shows on the page because we haven't written any code to show anything after it has been saved. So now we have to examine SQL Server.

Let's go to **View | SQL Server Object Explorer**. Right-click on the **dbo.Images** table icon and select **View Data**. As you can see in *Figure 26.5.9*, these are the images stored in a low-level form. This confirms that they've been saved:

Id	IMAGE
1	0xFFD8FFE000104A464946000101010060006000000FFE1005A4578696600004D4D002A000000080...
2	0xFFD8FFE000104A464946000101010060006000000FFE100664578696600004D4D002A000000080...
3	0xFFD8FFE000104A464946000101010060006000000FFE100664578696600004D4D002A000000080...
NULL	*NULL*

Figure 26.5.9: Images in the dbo.Images table stored in a low-level form

Perhaps, as an assignment for yourself, you can extract the files back from SQL Server and display them as images. This would be an interesting exercise.

Chapter review

For review, `Default.aspx` is the source code for the **Scan Folder** button, `ListBox`, and the button to **Save To SQL Server**. The code within the `Button1_Click...` block actually scans the folder and then displays the available image files; that is, the ones that at least ended in `.jpg`. Then, the code starting with the connection string runs when you want to save the files to SQL Server from the `ListBox` control.

The complete version of the `Default.aspx.cs` file for this chapter, including comments, is shown in the following code block:

```
//using is a directive
//System is a name space
//name space is a collection of features that our needs to run
using System;
using System.Data.SqlClient;
```

```
using System.IO;
//public means accessible anywhere
//partial means this class is split over multiple files
//class is a keyword and think of it as the outermost level of grouping
//:System.Web.UI.Page means our page inherits the features of a Page
public partial class _Default : System.Web.UI.Page
{
    protected void Button1_Click(object sender, EventArgs e)
    {
        //scan folder for all files ending in jpg
        var imgFiles = Directory.GetFiles(@"c:\data\", "*.jpg");
        foreach(var imgFile in imgFiles)
        {
            //add files to list box in page
            ListBox1.Items.Add(imgFile);
        }
    }
    protected void Button2_Click(object sender, EventArgs e)
    {
        //make a connection string
        string connString = @"Data Source=DESKTOP-4L6NSGO\SQLEXPRESS;
Initial Catalog=People;Integrated Security=True;Connect
Timeout=15;Encrypt=False;TrustServerCertificate=False;
ApplicationIntent=ReadWrite;MultiSubnetFailover=False";
        //make connection
        using (SqlConnection conn = new SqlConnection(connString))
        {
            //open connection
            conn.Open();
            foreach(var item in ListBox1.Items)
            {
                using (SqlCommand cmd =
                new SqlCommand
                ("insert into dbo.Images (image) values (@image)", conn))
                {
                    //read picture as bytes
                    byte[] picAsBytes = File.ReadAllBytes(item.ToString());
                    //add pictures to SQL server as bytes
                    cmd.Parameters.AddWithValue("@image", picAsBytes);
                    //perform the actual saving
                    cmd.ExecuteNonQuery();
                }
            }
        }
    }
}
```

Summary

In this chapter, you learned how to read files and then save them in SQL Server as images. You created a database table to store the files, stored image files on your hard drive, added namespaces, tested the scanning folder function, and built and made use of the connection string.

In the next chapter, we will take a look at the basics of XML, which stands for Extensible Markup Language.

27
Creating and Using an XML File

In this chapter, we will take a look at the basics of XML (short for Extensible Markup Language). Basically, it's a way of structuring information on the internet. A useful aspect of XML is that it's extensible, which means that you can create your own tags.

Adding a button to HTML

Crank up a project. The only thing to be put inside **<html>** is a single Button control. To do this, go to **Toolbox**, type but in the search field, and drag and drop the Button control below the line that begins with <form id=.... Change the text on the button to say Read XML.

Coding the XML

Now you will need a file that you can read. For this, go to **Solution Explorer** and right-click on the name of the website. Go to **Add** in the dropdown, and then select **Add New Item....** Type xml in the search field, and make sure that you choose **XML File** that says **Visual C#**. Your starting screen for XMLFile.xml should look like the one shown in *Figure 27.1.1*:

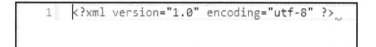

```
1    <?xml version="1.0" encoding="utf-8" ?>
```

Figure 27.1.1: The starting screen for XMLFile.xml

Now let's go through the creation of the code line-by-line, so that you can see what's exactly going on. Basically, just as in HTML, you have elements, nesting of elements, and attributes in XML.

First, imagine that you have a bookstore. In XML, you can create your own tags. So enter the following next:

```
<bookstore>
```

Notice that it automatically creates opening and closing tags: `<bookstore>` `</bookstore>`. Insert a few blank lines between these tags.

Of course, you have books in the book store, so enter the following next beneath the first `<bookstore>` tag:

```
<book type="eBook">
```

A book might be a traditional textbook, or it could be an eBook. So we will specify a type attribute, and set that equal to `eBook` for our first book.

Now let's talk about some of the elements stored under `<book type="eBook">`. One essential item, obviously, is the book title, so enter the following:

```
<booktitle>The Great Way</booktitle>
```

We will call the book, `The Great Way`.

In the next stage, naturally, you put in the author, so enter the following:

```
<author>Bob Jones</author>
```

So, our book was written by `Bob Jones`.

The last item, of course, is the price, which we'll say is $10.00 in this case, so enter the following:

```
<price>10.00</price>
```

This information provides the first book element, which as you can see consists of sub elements called `<booktitle>`, `<author>`, and `<price>`.

Now let's do one more book just for the sake of variety, as follows:

```
<book type="traditional">
    <booktitle>Happy People</booktitle>
    <author>Mary Jenkins</author>
    <price>11.00</price>
</book>
```

Our simple XML file is shown in the following code block:

```
<?xml version="1.0" encoding="utf-8" ?>
<bookstore>
    <book type="eBook">
        <booktitle>The Great Way</booktitle>
        <author>Bob Jones</author>
        <price>10.00</price>
    </book>
    <book type="traditional">
        <booktitle>Happy People</booktitle>
        <author>Mary Jenkins</author>
        <price>11.00</price>
    </book>
</bookstore>
```

Again, remember that XML is *Extensible,* because you can make your own tags, *Markup* because it has a structure similar to HTML, and, of course, it's a *Language*.

Now, right-click on the tab that says XMLFile.xml, and select **Copy Full Path** from the dropdown. We will make use of this path shortly. (If you hover your mouse over the XMLFile.xml tab, you can see the full path, however, it's long and difficult to remember, so it's better to right-click and select **Copy the Full Path**.)

Now click on the Default.aspx tab inside the HTML, switch to the **Design** view, and then double-click on the **Read XML** button. This brings up the event-handling code inside Default.aspx.cs. Delete the Page_Load stub. The relevant portion of the starting code for this project should look like that shown in *Figure 27.1.2*:

```
1     //using is a directive
2     //System is a name space
3     //name space is a collection of features that our needs to run
4     using System;
5                             //public means accessible anywhere
6                             //partial means this class is split over multiple files
7                             //class is a keyword and think of it as the outermost level of grouping
8                             //:System.Web.UI.Page means our page inherits the features of a Page
9     public partial class _Default : System.Web.UI.Page
10    {
11        protected void Button1_Click(object sender, EventArgs e)
12        {
13
14        }
15    }
16
```

Figure 27.1.2: The starting code for this project

Adding a namespace

Let's begin by adding a namespace. You need a new one, so enter the following after `using System` near the top of the file:

```
using System.Xml.Linq;
```

You will make use of this namespace as you code. (You can collapse all the code above the line that beings with `public partial class....`)

Loading the XML file into your program

In the next stage, enter the following within a set of curly braces beneath the line that begins with `protected void Button1_Click...`:

```
XElement fromFile = XElement.Load(@"C:\Users\towsi\Documents\Visual Studio
2015\WebSites\CSharpTemplateUpdated76143\XMLFile.xml");
```

You want to load `XElement fromFile`, so you say `XElement.Load()`. Then, within the parentheses, you put the @ symbol to make it a verbatim string, followed by double quotes. Now you need to make use of the path that you copied from `XMLFile.xml` so that you can load the XML from the file there. So, paste the path in between the set of `""` symbols. This will allow you to load the extensible markup file. Now hover your mouse over `XElement`. It says, **class System.Xml.Linq.XElement, Represents an XML element**.

Iterating over the contents of the XML file

Now, enter the following:

```
foreach(XElement childElement in fromFile.Elements())
```

If you hover your mouse over `Elements` at the end of this line, you can see that it's a function and it returns **IEnumerable**, so you can go over its contents, and each member within it is an element.

Displaying the results

Now you can display them, so enter the following between a set of curly braces:

First, you will need the book type. To get it, after you type `sampLabel.Text +=` `$"<br>Book Type:`, you say `{childElement.Attribute("type")`, and to get the value, you type `.Value}";`:

```
sampLabel.Text += $"<br>Book Type:{childElement.Attribute("type").Value}";
```

Now, to get the author you use `{childElement.Element("author")}";`, as follows:

```
sampLabel.Text += $"<br>{childElement.Element("author")}";
```

This is how you can get all of the elements out. At this stage, you can just copy and paste this line as it's pretty much the same thing for the book title and book price.

For book title, you say: `{childElement.Element("booktitle")}";`, as follows:

```
sampLabel.Text += $"<br>{childElement.Element("booktitle")}";
```

For price, you say: `{childElement.Element("price")}";`, as follows:

```
sampLabel.Text += $"<br>{childElement.Element("price")}";
```

At the end, to separate things out, you can use `"<br><hr/>";`, as follows:

```
sampLabel.Text += $"<br><hr/>";
```

Running the program

Now let's give it a go here, so crank it up in your browser. Remember, you are essentially reading XML into a web page. This is our objective here. Click on the **Read XML** button. The results are shown in Figure 27.1.3:

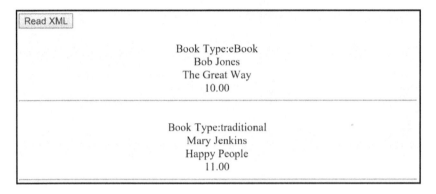

Figure 27.1.3: The results of running our program

The information is reported exactly as you entered it, as you would expect. Remember that the horizontal lines are present because you typed "`<br><hr/>`" inside the HTML page, which added a break and a horizontal rule or line.

This is how you can combine reading from an XML file, which is basically a collection of elements like the one in this project, many times nested. You can combine it with C#, and you can produce results.

Chapter review

The complete version of the `Default.aspx.cs` file for this chapter, including comments, is shown in the following code block:

```
//using is a directive
//System is a name space
//name space is a collection of features that our needs to run
using System;
using System.Xml.Linq;//needed for XElement
//public means accessible anywhere
//partial means this class is split over multiple files
//class is a keyword and think of it as the outermost level of grouping
//:System.Web.UI.Page means our page inherits the features of a Page
public partial class _Default : System.Web.UI.Page
```

```
{
    protected void Button1_Click(object sender, EventArgs e)
    {
        //load XML file into "fromFile" variable
        XElement fromFile = XElement.Load(@"C:\Users\towsi\Documents\Visual
Studio 2015\WebSites\CSharpTemplateUpdated76143\XMLFile.xml" );

        foreach(XElement childElement in fromFile.Elements())
        {
            //display value
            sampLabel.Text += $"<br>Book
Type:{childElement.Attribute("type").Value}";
            //display author
            sampLabel.Text += $"<br>{childElement.Element("author")}";
            //display book title
            sampLabel.Text += $"<br>{childElement.Element("booktitle")}";
            //display price
            sampLabel.Text += $"<br>{childElement.Element("price")}";
            //adds horizontal rule across the page
            sampLabel.Text += $"<br><hr/>";
        }
    }
}
```

Summary

In this chapter, you learned the basics of XML. You wrote XML code, loaded the resulting XML file into your program, iterated over the contents of the XML file, and wrote the code to display the results.

In the next chapter, you will learn how to write XML to a file and then view the results in Notepad and in Internet Explorer. So, you will come across lots of useful little things.

28

Creating XML Files with C#

In this chapter, you will learn how to write XML to a file and then view the results in Notepad and in Internet Explorer.

Adding a button to HTML

Start up a project, and put a button inside the HTML page. To do this, go to **View** | **Toolbox** (*Ctrl + Alt-X*), type but in the search field, and drag and drop the Button control below the line that begins with <form id=.... Change the text on the button to say Save File.

Next, go to the **Design** view. Double-click on the **Save File** button. This brings up the event handler inside Default.aspx.cs. Delete the Page_Load stub. Collapse all of the comments above and below using System;—you don't need them. The relevant portion of the starting code for this project should look like that in *Figure 28.2.1*:

```
1     // using is a directive ...
4     using System;
5     // public means accessible anywhere ...
9     public partial class _Default : System.Web.UI.Page
10    {
11        protected void Button1_Click(object sender, EventArgs e)
12        {
13
14        }
15    }
16
```

Figure 28.2.1: The starting code for this project

Adding namespaces

First, let's add some namespaces. Enter the following after `using System` near the top of the file:

```
using System.Xml;
using System.Diagnostics;
```

You need `using System.Diagnostics;` so that you can view a file in Internet Explorer and Notepad as soon as you create it.

Coding the XmlWriter settings

Next, you'll make the `XmlWriter` settings. So, enter the following between a set of curly braces beneath the line that begins with `protected void Button1_Click...`:

```
XmlWriterSettings settings = new XmlWriterSettings();
```

In this line, you make a setting object of this class, and then you'll set the feature. Enter the following next:

```
settings.Indent = true;
```

Enter the following below this line:

```
settings.IndentChars = "\t";
```

Here, `"\t"` is a tab.

Writing to the hard drive

Now, because the `XmlWriter` class uses the hard drive and the like, you need to enclose it within a `using` statement. So, enter the following next:

```
using (XmlWriter writer = XmlWriter.Create(@"c:\data\sampfile2.xml",
settings))
```

You'll create a file on the hard drive, `c:\data \sampfile2.xml`, and then you pass in the settings to be used. The settings object is passed as an argument to the `Create` function defined inside `XmlWriter`.

In the next stage, we'll actually write, so enter the following between a set of curly braces:

```
writer.WriteStartElement("bookstore");
writer.WriteEndElement();
```

With the second line, you immediately close the `WriteStartElement` method. We are adding a structure here.

Now you will add several lines of code between these two lines. Start by writing an attribute string, as follows:

```
writer.WriteAttributeString("name", "Tom's Book Store");
```

Next, you'll make another element. Here, it will be helpful if you indent the code, which suggests that the `book` element is under the `bookstore` element. For this, enter the following:

```
writer.WriteStartElement("book");
```

The element to be written is `book`. Enter the following next:

```
writer.WriteStartElement("bookauthor");
```

Now let's do the following to close this:

```
writer.WriteEndElement();
```

You do this to keep the end and the start in pairs.

Now, within this (above the `WriteEndElement` line), you can write another element. In this line, you'll include the specific book author. Again, you will write a string, and the author's name will be the value. Enter the following:

```
writer.WriteString("John Smith");
```

Here, keep an eye out because `WriteAttribute` is different from `WriteString`. `WriteString` goes between the tags, while `WriteAttribute` gives an attribute, so it's different. This is sufficient for our purposes.

Formatting the results

Now you want to make sure that the results look decent. So, outside the closing curly brace beneath the last `WriteEndElement` line, enter the following:

```
Process.Start("notepad.exe", @"c:\data\sampfile2.xml");
```

You'll view the results in Notepad, and then you'll need the path of the file, so copy that from the preceding `using` line, `c:\data\sampfile2.xml`, and paste it into this line.

Let's do one more now. Basically, just repeat this line and change where it says `notepad.exe` to `iexplore.exe`, as follows, in order to indicate that Internet Explorer should be used next:

```
Process.Start("iexplore.exe", @"c:\data\sampfile2.xml");
```

Running the program

Now let's crank this up in your browser and take a look at the results. Click on the **Save File** button, and you'll see what it looks like in Internet Explorer:

```
<?xml version="1.0" encoding="UTF-8"?>
- <bookstore name="Tom's Book Store">
  - <book>
        <bookauthor>John Smith</bookauthor>
    </book>
</bookstore>
```

Figure 28.2.2: The results of running the program as they appear in Internet Explorer

You can see that it's got structure, and the results are even collapsible, as indicated by the - symbol before the XML tag, and of course expandable as well. The name of the book store is Tom's Book Store, which is the attribute, and then, John Smith, the author, which is written as a string between the book author tags or element.

Likewise, in Notepad, it looks like the screen shown in *Figure 28.2.3*, with correctly formatted XML:

Figure 28.2.3: The results of running the program as they appear in Notepad

So, these are the basics of doing these operations.

Chapter review

The complete version of the `Default.aspx.cs` file for this chapter, including comments, is shown in the following code block:

```
//using is a directive
//System is a name space
//name space is a collection of features that our needs to run
using System;
using System.Xml;
using System.Diagnostics;
//public means accessible anywhere
//partial means this class is split over multiple files
//class is a keyword and think of it as the outermost level of grouping
//:System.Web.UI.Page means our page inherits the features of a Page
public partial class _Default : System.Web.UI.Page
{
    protected void Button1_Click(object sender, EventArgs e)
    {
        //make a setting object
        XmlWriterSettings settings = new XmlWriterSettings();
        //set indent to true
        settings.Indent = true;
        //use tabs for indenting
        settings.IndentChars = "\t";
        //create file to write to
        using (XmlWriter writer =
        XmlWriter.Create(@"c:\data\sampfile2.xml", settings))
```

```
        {
            //outermost element
            writer.WriteStartElement("bookstore");
            //attribute of book store
            writer.WriteAttributeString("name", "Tom's Book Store");
                //new element called book
                writer.WriteStartElement("book");
                    //new element called author
                    writer.WriteStartElement("bookauthor");
                    //this goes between the author tags
                    writer.WriteString("John Smith");
                writer.WriteEndElement();
            writer.WriteEndElement();
        }
        //priview the files in notepad and internet explorer
        Process.Start("notepad.exe", @"c:\data\sampfile2.xml");
        Process.Start("iexplore.exe", @"c:\data\sampfile2.xml");
    }
}
```

Summary

In this chapter, you learned how to write XML to a file and then view the results in Notepad and Internet Explorer. You coded the `XmlWriter` settings and wrote the code to write to the hard drive as well as to format the results.

In the next chapter, you will learn how to combine LINQ and XML to make something more practical.

29
Querying XML Documents with LINQ

In this chapter, you will learn how to combine LINQ and XML to make something more practical.

Adding a text box and a button to HTML

Crank up a project, and inside **\<html\>**, the first thing that you need to do is adding a `TextBox` control. To do this, go to **View** | **Toolbox**, type `tex` in the search field, and drag and drop the `TextBox` below the line that begins with `<form id=`.... Type `Enter Value`: at the beginning of the line, so that it looks like the following:

```
Enter Value:<asp:TextBoxID="TextBox1" runat="server"></asp:TextBox>
```

So, you'll have a box; enter a value into the box, and then you'll get a result. You'll scan an XML document to select items that are above a certain value, $50 or $60, for example. This is our objective; in other words, to make a searchable page.

Next, you'll insert a button into **\<html\>**. So again, go to **Toolbox**, type `but` in the search field, and drag and drop the `Button` control beneath the preceding line. Change the text on the `Button` control to say something easy such as `Search`, as follows:

```
<asp:ButtonID="Button1" runat="server" Text="Search" />
```

Next, go to the **Design** view. It looks like the screenshot shown in *Figure 29.3.1*:

Figure 29.3.1: The interface of this project in Design view

Double-click on the **Search** button. This brings up the `Default.aspx.cs` file. Delete the `Page_Load` stub. Collapse all of the comments above and below `using System;`—you don't need them. The relevant portion of the starting code for this project should look like *Figure 29.3.2*:

```
1     // using is a directive ...
4    using ...
7     // public means accessible anywhere ...
11   public partial class _Default : System.Web.UI.Page
12   {
13        protected void Button1_Click(object sender, EventArgs e)
14        {
15
16        }
17   }
18
```

Figure 29.3.2: The starting code for this project

There's a bit of interesting code in this one—very practical. Do keep in mind that whenever you learn a programming language, the simple truth is that what you do in real life is far more challenging than anything that you will see in a book like this.

Adding namespaces

Now let's add some namespaces. Enter the following under `using System` near the top of the file:

```
using System.Xml.Linq;
using System.Linq;
```

So, we have a bridge between XML and LINQ—that's our objective here.

Clearing the output

First, you need to clear label every time so that the output does not accumulate on the label. So, enter the following between a set of curly braces under the line that begins with `protected void Button1_Click...`:

```
sampLabel.Text = "";
```

Building an element tree

Next, we will make an element tree using the following syntax:

```
XElement store = new XElement("store",
```

In this line, `store` is the name of the tree. Basically, it holds information about products. Remember, if you want to know where something comes from, just hover your mouse over it. Thus, if you hover your mouse over `XElement` at the beginning of this line, the tooltip shows that **it does not come from the XML namespace. Rather, it comes from the Xml.Linq namespace**.

Next, you'll put other elements inside `store`. So, insert several blank lines right before the closing parentheses with the semicolon, and now you'll stack things inside it.

 Be sure to put the comma in after `store` in the preceding line. When you type the comma, take a look at the tooltip. Do you see where it says **params object[] content**? This means that there are a variable number of arguments there which you can specify to build up the tree. Remember, **params** means that you can specify a variable number of arguments.

First, we'll have a new element inside the store called `shoes`. So, indent the following line:

```
new XElement("shoes",
```

Next, indent the following lines further in:

```
new XElement("brand", "Nike", new XAttribute("price", "65")),
```

Here, you say `new XAttribute`, just to show you that it's possible. The attribute will be the `price`, and the value will be, for example, `$65`. You close that attribute and close the element with a comma.

Now since you will repeat this, copy this line and paste it below, changing the brand name to `Stacy Adams` and the price to `$120`, as follows:

```
new XElement("brand", "Stacy Adams", new XAttribute("price", "120")),
```

Let's repeat this one more time. So once again, copy this line and paste it underneath, changing the brand name to `Florsheim` and the price to `$90`, as follows:

```
new XElement("brand", "Florsheim", new XAttribute("price", "90"))));
```

Note that at the end of the last line here, you close with four parentheses and a semicolon. You must be extremely careful about this. You must make sure that everything is matching. So, you have a Store, and then you have a Shoes department, and within the Shoes department you carry different Brands: Nike, Stacy Adams, and Florsheim.

Saving the store XML file

Now, it's good to be able to write this out to a file to confirm that the structure is interpreted in that it appears the way it's supposed to look. So enter the following next, aligning the indent with the preceding `XElement store...` line:

```
store.Save(@"c:\data\storefile.xml");
```

Here, `store.Save()` is a nice function that you can call directly. You save this to a file, in this case: `(@"c:\data \storefile.xml");`.

Testing the program

Before doing anything else, let's confirm that this will work as expected and that it generates a good-looking XML file. So, open it up in your browser and click on the **Search** button, as shown in *Figure 29.3.3*:

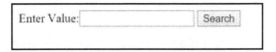

Figure 29.3.3: The interface displayed when testing the program at present

Of course, nothing shows right now, because you haven't coded that part yet. However, if you do a directory listing of `c:\data`, there is the saved file, `storefile.xml`, as shown in *Figure 29.3.4*:

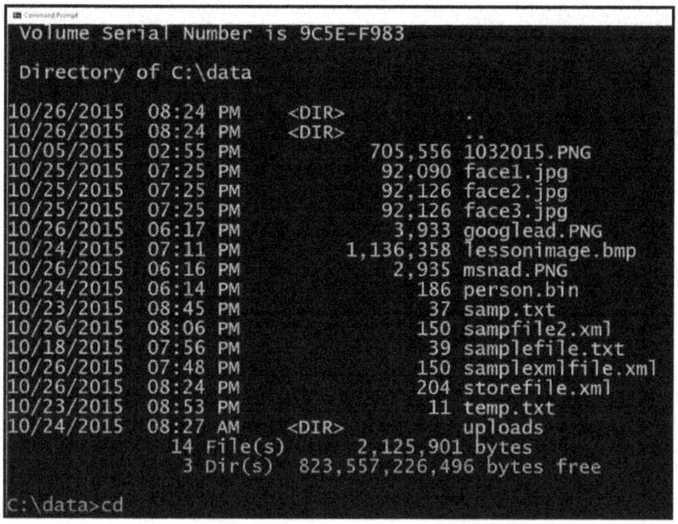

Figure 29.3.4: The file storefile.xml is saved in the c:\data directory

If you open this file in Notepad by typing `notepad.exe storefile.xml` at the `c:\data>` prompt, you will see the result shown in *Figure 29.3.5*:

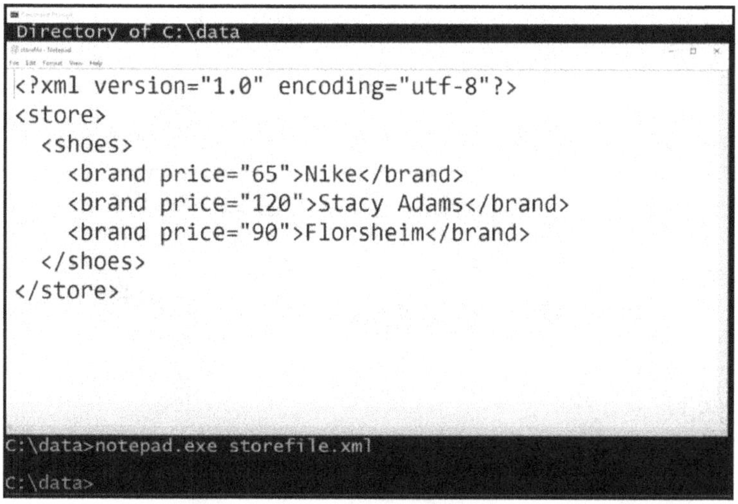

Figure 29.3.5: The file storefile.xml opened in Notepad

This looks very good. You have a `store` element, and then within the `store` element you have `shoes`, and within `shoes` you have brands `Nike`, `Stacy Adams`, and `Florsheim`, and each shoe carries a price: $65, $120, and $90, respectively. So, it looks like a good file, and it is sufficient for our purposes. (In real life, believe me that these things are a lot more complicated.)

Searching for items that meet a specific criteria

Next, enter the following beneath the line that began with `store.Save...`, to search for shoes:

```
var shoeSearch = from shoes in
store.Descendants("shoes").Descendants("brand")
```

Here, `var shoeSearch` is a combination of LINQ and XML.

Next, type `where (decimal)`, which is used to convert to a decimal value, and that the price is greater than a value entered by the user:

```
where (decimal)shoes.Attribute("price") >decimal.Parse(TextBox1.Text)
```

Selecting among the items that meet the search criteria

Once those shoes are found, you can select among them, as follows:

```
select shoes;
```

If you hover your mouse over the first use of `Descendants` in the preceding line, it tells you that it returns **IEnumerable**. The tooltip says that it **Returns a filtered collection of the descendant elements for this document or element, in document order**.

Also, if you hover your mouse over the second use of `Descendants`, you'll see that it goes by the brand. Once you're there at that level, then you can, for example, hover your mouse over the `price` attribute in the preceding line that begins with `where...`, and then compare this attribute against the value specified by the user. So, it's as if you're traversing it from the outside to the inside until you get to the price attribute and then, at that stage, you make the comparison of that value to the one entered by the user.

Displaying the results

Enter the following line next to display all of the shoe brands and prices that were selected by the search:

```
foreach(XElement shoeBrand in shoeSearch)
```

Finally, enter the following between a set of curly braces beneath the preceding line:

```
sampLabel.Text +=
$"<br>Brand:{shoeBrand}<br>Price:{(decimal)shoeBrand.Attribute("price"):C}"
;
```

In this line, there could be multiple values, so you append. Note that we place the `<br>` tags to push each result down to the next line. To display the price, you say `(decimal)` to convert to a decimal value, and then after `shoeBrand.Attribute("price")`, you convert that to a currency format with `:C`. So that's all of the code. It's very important to type all of this in. The best way to learn is by doing, not simply by opening a previously prepared file and running it.

Running the program

Now open your browser one last time, input a value of, say, 45, and click on the **Search** button. It should return all of the shoes, right, because the prices are all higher than that, as shown in *Figure 29.3.6*:

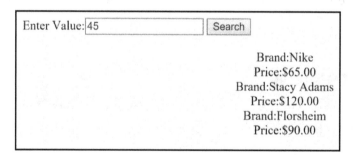

Figure 29.3.6: All of the shoes and prices are displayed, as the value entered is less than the price of any of the shoes

Now enter 100 as the value, and click on the **Search** button again. In this case, it only returns the **Stacy Adams** shoe, which is priced at **$120**, as shown in *Figure 29.3.7*:

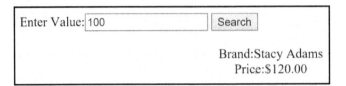

Figure 29.3.7: Only the Stacy Adams shoe is returned, as it is priced above $100

Let's do one more. Enter 85, and click on the **Search** button once again. As shown in *Figure 29.3.8*, it returns the **Stacy Adams** and **Florsheim** shoes, as both of these are priced at $85 or above:

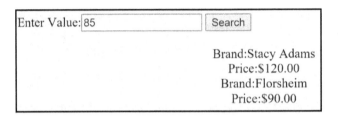

Figure 29.3.8: the Stacy Adams and Florsheim shoes are returned, as both are priced at $85 or more

There you go. So that's working as expected. We also generated a beautiful-looking XML file using the entire XElement construction that you wrote in order for this program to work correctly.

Chapter review

The complete version of the Default.aspx.cs file for this chapter, including comments, is shown in the following code block:

```
//using is a directive
//System is a name space
//name space is a collection of features that our needs to run
using System;
using System.Xml.Linq;
using System.Linq;
//public means accessible anywhere
//partial means this class is split over multiple files
//class is a keyword and think of it as the outermost level of grouping
```

```
//:System.Web.UI.Page means our page inherits the features of a Page
public partial class _Default : System.Web.UI.Page
{
    protected void Button1_Click(object sender, EventArgs e)
    {
        //clear label on every button click so stuff does not accumulate
        sampLabel.Text = "";
        //create a nice XML tree structure for searching: store is the
        //root, inside that is shoes,
        //and then under shoes are three different brands
        XElement store = new XElement("store",
                        new XElement("shoes",
                        new XElement("brand","Nike",
                        new XAttribute("price","65")),
                        new XElement("brand", "Stacy Adams",
                        new XAttribute("price","120")),
                        new XElement("brand", "Florsheim",
                        new XAttribute("price","90")))));
        //save file to drive to confirm it looks like healthy XML
        store.Save(@"c:\data\storefile.xml");
        //search down to the level of the price attribute, and compare that
        //value against the value entered in the search box by the user
        var shoeSearch = from shoes in
store.Descendants("shoes").Descendants("brand")
        where (decimal)shoes.Attribute("price") >
decimal.Parse(TextBox1.Text)select shoes;
        //display all the shoe brands, and the prices
        foreach(XElement shoeBrand in shoeSearch)
        {
            sampLabel.Text +=
$"<br>Brand:{shoeBrand}<br>Price:{(decimal)shoeBrand.Attribute("price"):C}"
;
        }
    }
}
```

Summary

In this chapter, you learned how to combine LINQ and XML to make something more practical. You built an element tree and wrote the code to save the store XML file, to search for items that met a specific criterion, and to select among the items found those that met the search criteria.

Index

www.ingramcontent.com/pod-product-compliance
Lightning Source LLC
Chambersburg PA
CBHW080626060326
40690CB00021B/4824